Name : _______________________

Subtraction Worksheets

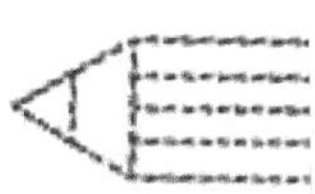

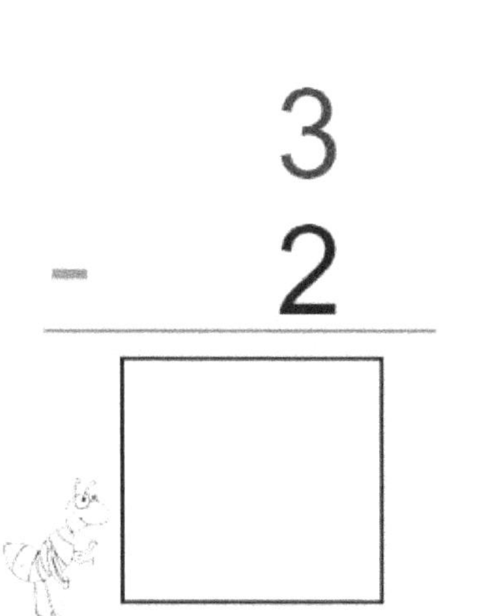
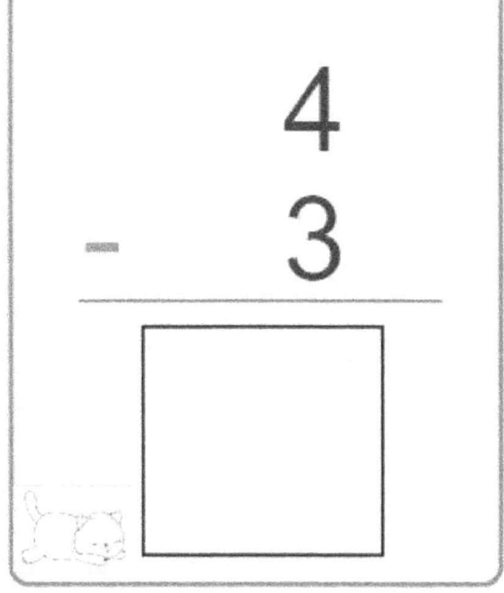

$$3 - 2 =$$

$$3 - 2 =$$

$$4 - 3 =$$

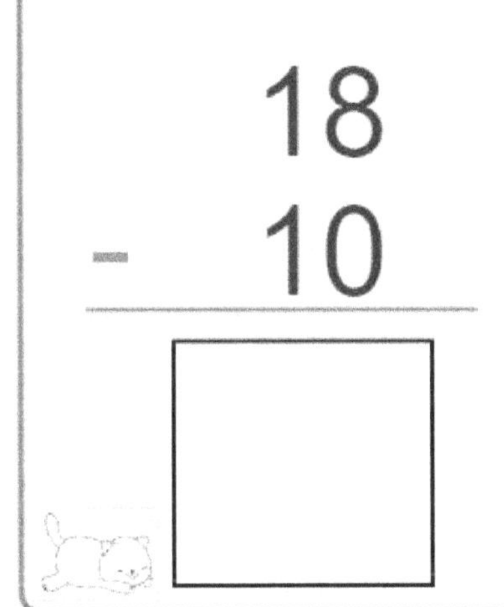
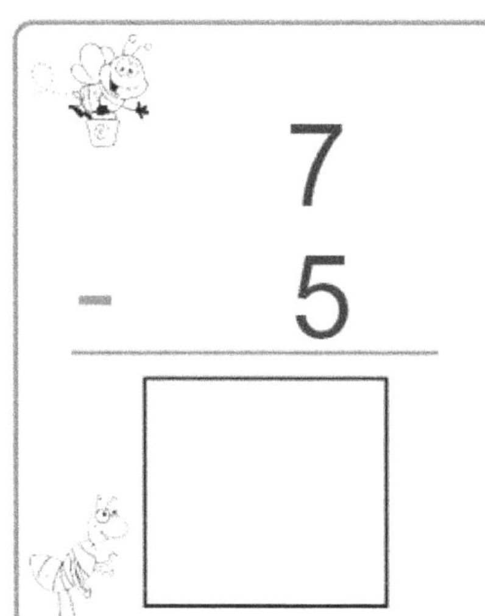
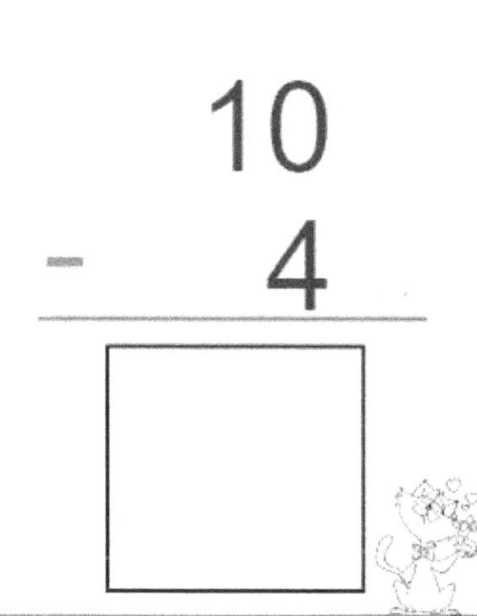

$$18 - 10 =$$

$$7 - 5 =$$

$$10 - 4 =$$

$$14 - 4 =$$

$$1 - 1 =$$

$$10 - 1 =$$

Math Made Easy....

Name : _______________________________

Direction: Use the picture to help you find the answer.

1 2 3 4 5 6 7 8 9 10

20 - 10 = _____

6 - 4 = _____

14 - 2 = _____

5 - 3 = _____

12 - 4 = _____

1 - 1 = _____

14 - 8 = _____

6 - 3 = _____

5 - 4 = _____

16 - 10 = _____

Subtraction Worksheets

9	4	5
− 6	− 3	− 3

2	1	1
− 1	− 1	− 1

15	15	11
− 5	− 6	− 7

  Math Made Easy....

Name : _______________________________

Direction: Use the picture to help you find the answer.

| 1 | 2 | 3 | 4 | 5 | 6 | 7 | 8 | 9 | 10 |

17 - 10 = ___

17 - 12 = ___

18 - 13 = ___

2 - 1 = ___

7 - 6 = ___

9 - 3 = ___

14 - 1 = ___

18 - 13 = ___

1 - 1 = ___

12 - 5 = ___

Subtraction Worksheets

20 − 18 =	17 − 12 =	3 − 1 =
6 − 5 =	20 − 19 =	15 − 1 =
7 − 4 =	15 − 6 =	3 − 2 =

Name : _______________________________

Direction: Use the picture to help you find the answer.

1   2   3   4   5   6   7   8   9   10

17 - 12 = ____

17 - 1 = ____

10 - 5 = ____

4 - 1 = ____

12 - 4 = ____

1 - 1 = ____

1 - 1 = ____

4 - 2 = ____

12 - 10 = ____

18 - 4 = ____

Subtraction Worksheets

6	20	13
− 5	− 2	− 7

18	10	5
− 2	− 5	− 2

1	14	16
− 1	− 1	− 11

Name : ___________________________

Direction: Use the picture to help you find the answer.

1 2 3 4 5 6 7 8 9 10

6 - 3 = ____

16 - 4 = ____

1 - 1 = ____

6 - 3 = ____

3 - 1 = ____

16 - 11 = ____

11 - 10 = ____

12 - 6 = ____

19 - 10 = ____

14 - 3 = ____

Subtraction Worksheets

8 - 1	1 - 1	9 - 8
12 - 7	1 - 1	18 - 6
16 - 10	9 - 8	1 - 1

1 - 1 = _____

2 - 1 = _____

12 - 7 = _____

20 - 10 = _____

17 - 7 = _____

16 - 15 = _____

16 - 3 = _____

18 - 3 = _____

7 - 6 = _____

2 - 1 = _____

Subtraction Worksheets

| 13 | 7 | 10 |
| - 8 | - 1 | - 3 |

| 14 | 9 | 4 |
| - 9 | - 3 | - 3 |

| 10 | 1 | 6 |
| - 2 | - 1 | - 2 |

 Math Made Easy.... 

Name : _______________________________

Direction: Use the picture to help you find the answer.

1   2   3   4   5   6   7   8   9   10

4 - 3 = ____

14 - 3 = ____

11 - 8 = ____

9 - 1 = ____

11 - 5 = ____

20 - 15 = ____

8 - 7 = ____

6 - 3 = ____

19 - 17 = ____

12 - 10 = ____

Name : ________________________

Subtraction Worksheets

6 − 5	10 − 5	8 − 1
6 − 5	1 − 1	9 − 2
19 − 17	20 − 2	4 − 3

Math Made Easy....

Name : ________________________

Direction: Use the picture to help you find the answer.

1 2 3 4 5 6 7 8 9 10

7 - 6 = ___	13 - 7 = ___
9 - 2 = ___	10 - 5 = ___
16 - 14 = ___	10 - 3 = ___
1 - 1 = ___	1 - 1 = ___
16 - 15 = ___	2 - 1 = ___

Subtraction Worksheets

15
− 7

4
− 3

16
− 1

3
− 2

7
− 6

2
− 1

14
− 8

14
− 5

19
− 16

Math Made Easy....

Name : _______________________________

Direction: Use the picture to help you find the answer.

1 2 3 4 5 6 7 8 9 10

16 - 3 = ___

11 - 8 = ___

4 - 2 = ___

6 - 4 = ___

9 - 4 = ___

17 - 13 = ___

17 - 16 = ___

5 - 1 = ___

18 - 3 = ___

1 - 1 = ___

Subtraction Worksheets

7 − 6	7 − 5	14 − 12
6 − 5	15 − 7	9 − 2
6 − 3	17 − 10	14 − 12

Math Made Easy....

Name : ________________________________

Direction: Use the picture to help you find the answer.

| 1 | 2 | 3 | 4 | 5 | 6 | 7 | 8 | 9 | 10 |

$5 - 4 =$ ___

$6 - 1 =$ ___

$11 - 2 =$ ___

$15 - 5 =$ ___

$9 - 6 =$ ___

$7 - 4 =$ ___

$14 - 5 =$ ___

$14 - 1 =$ ___

$14 - 5 =$ ___

$2 - 1 =$ ___

Subtraction Worksheets

Name : ______________

1 − 1 =	14 − 12 =	6 − 4 =
11 − 3 =	15 − 9 =	9 − 4 =
16 − 2 =	18 − 8 =	15 − 9 =

Math Made Easy....

Name : _______________________________

Direction: Use the picture to help you find the answer.

1   2   3   4   5   6   7   8   9   10

8 - 7 = _____

18 - 5 = _____

10 - 4 = _____

15 - 11 = _____

17 - 14 = _____

6 - 2 = _____

1 - 1 = _____

11 - 2 = _____

10 - 3 = _____

7 - 2 = _____

Name : _______________________

Subtraction Worksheets

3 − 1	12 − 4	2 − 1
13 − 8	1 − 1	4 − 3
18 − 14	8 − 6	7 − 6

Math Made Easy....

Name : _______________________________

Direction: Use the picture to help you find the answer.

1   2   3   4   5   6   7   8   9   10

5 - 1 =	11 - 9 =
3 - 1 =	2 - 1 =
10 - 4 =	12 - 5 =
2 - 1 =	13 - 7 =
17 - 1 =	1 - 1 =

Subtraction Worksheets

16 − 14	

| 3
− 2 | |

| 5
− 2 | |

| 8
− 5 | |

| 11
− 7 | |

| 15
− 14 | |

| 1
− 1 | |

| 16
− 5 | |

| 18
− 5 | |

Math Made Easy....

Name : _______________________________

Direction: Use the picture to help you find the answer.

| 1 | 2 | 3 | 4 | 5 | 6 | 7 | 8 | 9 | 10 |

17 - 9 = ____

1 - 1 = ____

3 - 2 = ____

16 - 7 = ____

17 - 3 = ____

1 - 1 = ____

10 - 8 = ____

1 - 1 = ____

4 - 3 = ____

17 - 11 = ____

Subtraction Worksheets

19 − 13	3 − 1	18 − 5
10 − 6	2 − 1	3 − 2
5 − 1	9 − 5	20 − 19

Math Made Easy....

Direction: Use the picture to help you find the answer.

16 - 13 = _____

7 - 5 = _____

18 - 11 = _____

15 - 3 = _____

18 - 2 = _____

13 - 6 = _____

17 - 10 = _____

4 - 1 = _____

14 - 9 = _____

7 - 4 = _____

Subtraction Worksheets

4 − 2	16 − 6	2 − 1
9 − 1	20 − 12	20 − 11
6 − 4	11 − 1	8 − 6

Name : _______________________

Direction: Use the picture to help you find the answer.

1   2   3   4   5   6   7   8   9   10

4 − 3 = ___	20 − 1 = ___
3 − 1 = ___	13 − 2 = ___
16 − 1 = ___	20 − 2 = ___
17 − 14 = ___	19 − 7 = ___
10 − 4 = ___	10 − 8 = ___

Subtraction Worksheets

11	
− 10	

18	
− 9	

4	
− 3	

13	
− 2	

13	
− 9	

1	
− 1	

10	
− 1	

2	
− 1	

13	
− 6	

Name : ________________________

Direction: Use the picture to help you find the answer.

1 2 3 4 5 6 7 8 9 10

7 - 6 = ____	12 - 7 = ____
1 - 1 = ____	17 - 5 = ____
13 - 12 = ____	19 - 3 = ____
3 - 1 = ____	15 - 7 = ____
12 - 3 = ____	12 - 7 = ____

Subtraction Worksheets

5	15	14
− 1	− 2	− 8

12	4	6
− 7	− 1	− 3

18	7	20
− 2	− 5	− 19

 Math Made Easy....

Name : _______________________________________

Direction: Use the picture to help you find the answer.

1   2   3   4   5   6   7   8   9   10

10 - 5 _____

1 - 1 _____

16 - 2 _____

9 - 4 _____

2 - 1 _____

2 - 1 _____

17 - 9 _____

8 - 4 _____

15 - 3 _____

16 - 13 _____

Subtraction Worksheets

16	19	15
− 12	− 13	− 1

7	13	7
− 1	− 5	− 4

13	8	8
− 8	− 6	− 5

Name : _______________________________

Direction: Use the picture to help you find the answer.

| 1 | 2 | 3 | 4 | 5 | 6 | 7 | 8 | 9 | 10 |

16 - 7 = ___

12 - 9 = ___

3 - 2 = ___

14 - 11 = ___

4 - 2 = ___

7 - 3 = ___

16 - 8 = ___

19 - 15 = ___

17 - 16 = ___

12 - 5 = ___

10 − 1	2 − 1	13 − 12
12 − 10	13 − 6	17 − 5
11 − 9	4 − 3	3 − 1

Name : ___________________________________

Direction: Use the picture to help you find the answer.

1   2   3   4   5   6   7   8   9   10

10 − 5 = ____	16 − 9 = ____
19 − 7 = ____	12 − 5 = ____
10 − 5 = ____	13 − 8 = ____
15 − 11 = ____	18 − 1 = ____
19 − 1 = ____	4 − 3 = ____

Subtraction Worksheets

9	7	2
− 5	− 2	− 1

14	8	10
− 7	− 7	− 5

1	18	6
− 1	− 9	− 3

Name : _______________________________

Direction: Use the picture to help you find the answer.

1   2   3   4   5   6   7   8   9   10

11 - 5 = ___	10 - 7 = ___
9 - 1 = ___	10 - 8 = ___
4 - 3 = ___	17 - 14 = ___
2 - 1 = ___	20 - 18 = ___
19 - 4 = ___	8 - 4 = ___

Name : _______________

Subtraction Worksheets

| 2 |
| - 1 |

| 6 |
| - 3 |

| 4 |
| - 1 |

| 6 |
| - 4 |

| 12 |
| - 9 |

| 13 |
| - 9 |

| 7 |
| - 6 |

| 11 |
| - 10 |

| 13 |
| - 1 |

Math Made Easy....

Name : _______________________________

Direction: Use the picture to help you find the answer.

1   2   3   4   5   6   7   8   9   10

15 - 8 = _______

1 - 1 = _______

1 - 1 = _______

5 - 3 = _______

8 - 3 = _______

1 - 1 = _______

18 - 2 = _______

19 - 9 = _______

13 - 11 = _______

17 - 4 = _______

Subtraction Worksheets

18		4		17
− 13		− 3		− 16

19		1		10
− 2		− 1		− 2

10		19		11
− 3		− 14		− 8

Math Made Easy....

Direction: Use the picture to help you find the answer.

1   2   3   4   5   6   7   8   9   10

20 - 17 = ___	6 - 1 = ___
4 - 3 = ___	20 - 17 = ___
17 - 16 = ___	2 - 1 = ___
14 - 12 = ___	7 - 1 = ___
9 - 7 = ___	2 - 1 = ___

Subtraction Worksheets

18	16	17
− 7	− 4	− 15

20	1	9
− 1	− 1	− 6

2	20	7
− 1	− 5	− 2

Name : _______________________________

Direction: Use the picture to help you find the answer.

1   2   3   4   5   6   7   8   9   10

10 - 1 = ___

8 - 3 = ___

18 - 12 = ___

2 - 1 = ___

4 - 2 = ___

14 - 12 = ___

8 - 2 = ___

6 - 2 = ___

2 - 1 = ___

13 - 7 = ___

Subtraction Worksheets

20 − 11 ☐	1 − 1 ☐	18 − 14 ☐
15 − 13 ☐	11 − 8 ☐	9 − 7 ☐
15 − 1 ☐	9 − 8 ☐	16 − 15 ☐

Name : _______________________________

Direction: Use the picture to help you find the answer.

1 2 3 4 5 6 7 8 9 10

16 - 10 = ____

4 - 2 = ____

1 - 1 = ____

1 - 1 = ____

4 - 3 = ____

13 - 7 = ____

2 - 1 = ____

14 - 1 = ____

13 - 8 = ____

16 - 13 = ____

Subtraction Worksheets

20 − 9	16 − 6	14 − 2
8 − 4	12 − 7	1 − 1
4 − 2	7 − 5	18 − 2

Math Made Easy....

1　2　3　4　5　6　7　8　9　10

14 - 1 = ____	20 - 15 = ____
16 - 4 = ____	18 - 9 = ____
14 - 3 = ____	13 - 12 = ____
1 - 1 = ____	13 - 1 = ____
2 - 1 = ____	15 - 2 = ____

Subtraction Worksheets

17 − 12	9 − 4	7 − 6
8 − 1	1 − 1	12 − 2
2 − 1	13 − 8	20 − 7

Name : _______________________________

Direction: Use the picture to help you find the answer.

1 2 3 4 5 6 7 8 9 10

20 - 15 = _____

10 - 9 = _____

10 - 8 = _____

17 - 9 = _____

15 - 5 = _____

7 - 6 = _____

8 - 4 = _____

11 - 7 = _____

11 - 10 = _____

12 - 5 = _____

Subtraction Worksheets

4 − 1	1 − 1	5 − 4
3 − 1	2 − 1	19 − 14
7 − 3	18 − 6	19 − 17

18 + 1	19 + 7	17 + 9
13 + 15	3 + 9	9 + 2
2 + 18	19 + 11	12 + 9

Addition Worksheets

18 + 1	19 + 7	17 + 9
13 + 15	3 + 9	9 + 2
2 + 18	19 + 11	12 + 9

Name : ________________________

Direction: Add the number of images in each box and
write the answer in the last box.

3
+ 2

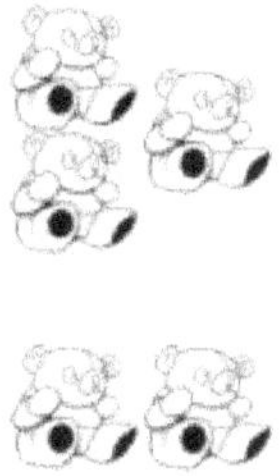

Answer

2
+ 8

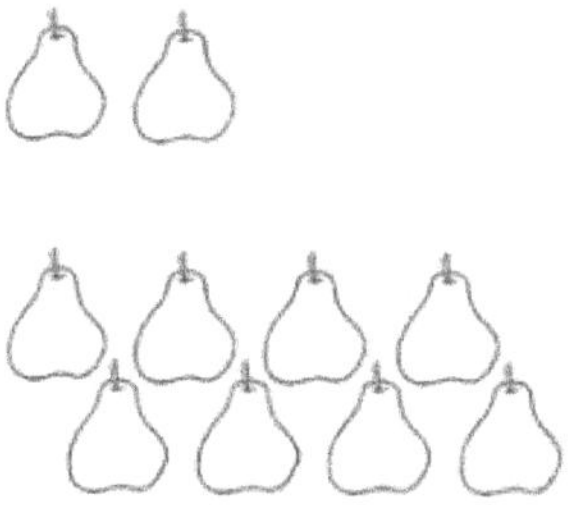

Answer

5
+ 5

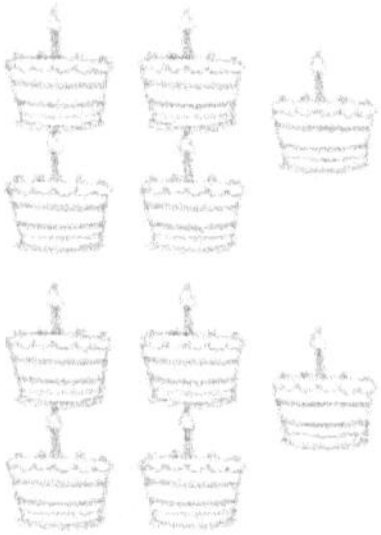

Answer

6
+ 6

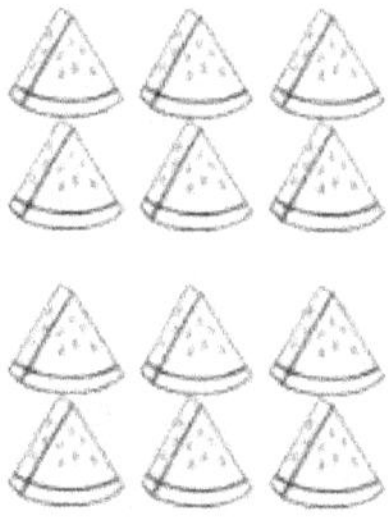

Answer

6
+ 3

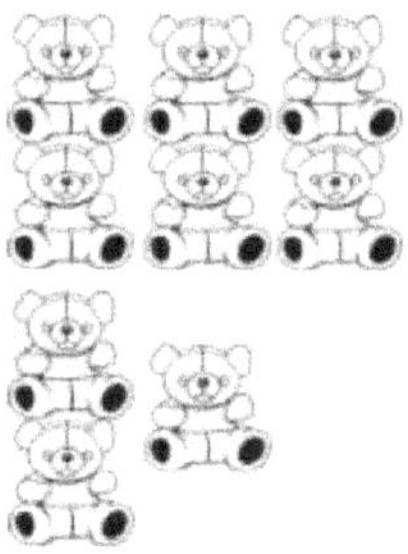

Answer

1
+ 1

Answer

Addition Worksheets

$$9 + 11 = \square$$

$$14 + 10 = \square$$

$$4 + 2 = \square$$

$$18 + 3 = \square$$

$$5 + 17 = \square$$

$$17 + 15 = \square$$

$$2 + 4 = \square$$

$$3 + 14 = \square$$

$$16 + 6 = \square$$

Name : _______________________

Direction: Add the number of images in each box and write the answer in the last box.

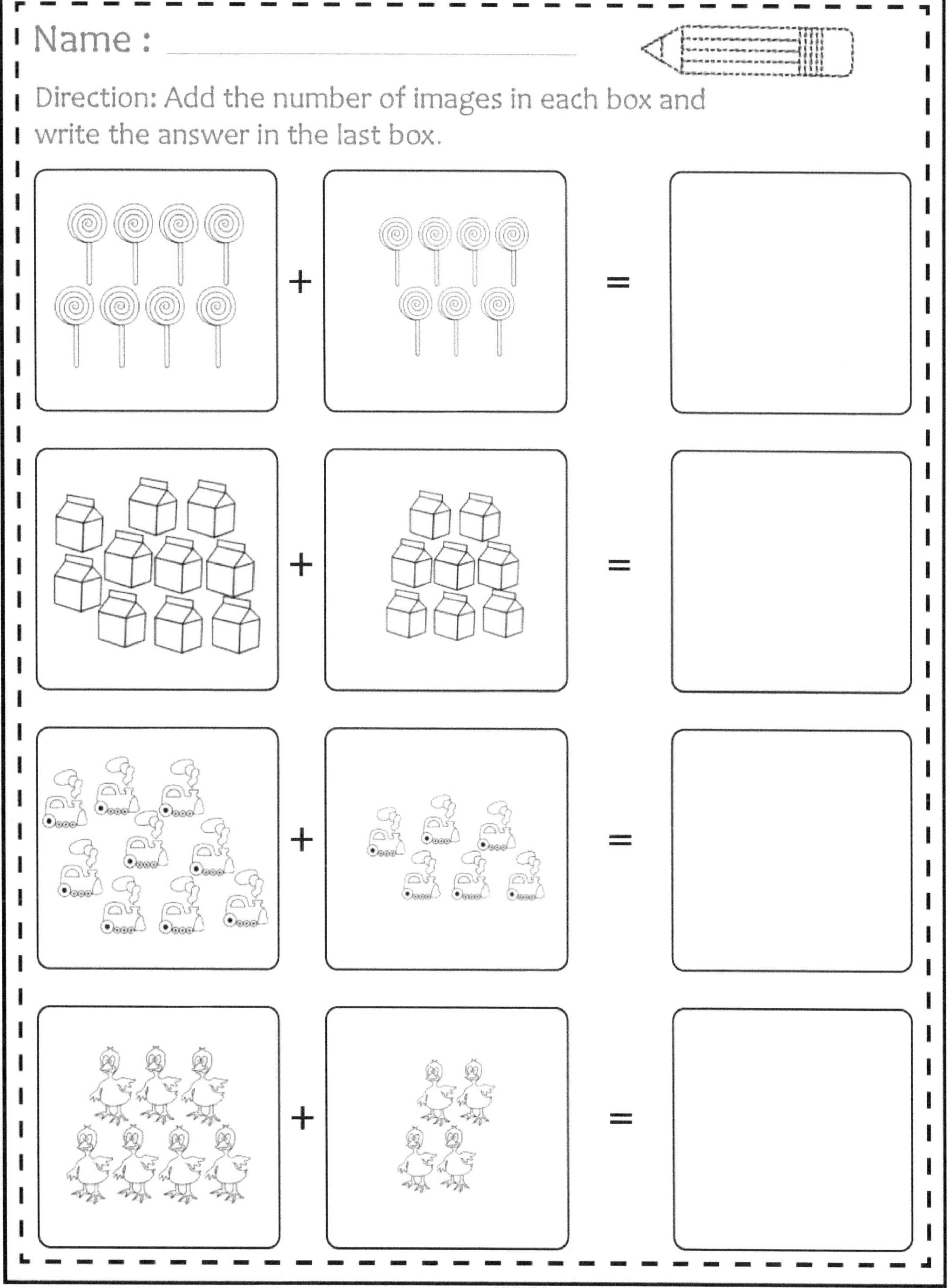

Name : _______________

Addition Worksheets

2
+ 7

☐ Answer

3
+ 2

☐ Answer

3
+ 5

☐ Answer

2
+ 4

☐ Answer

4
+ 7

☐ Answer

1
+ 1

☐ Answer

Addition Worksheets

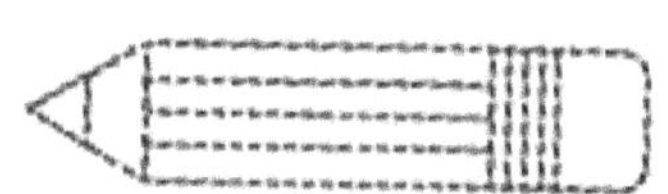

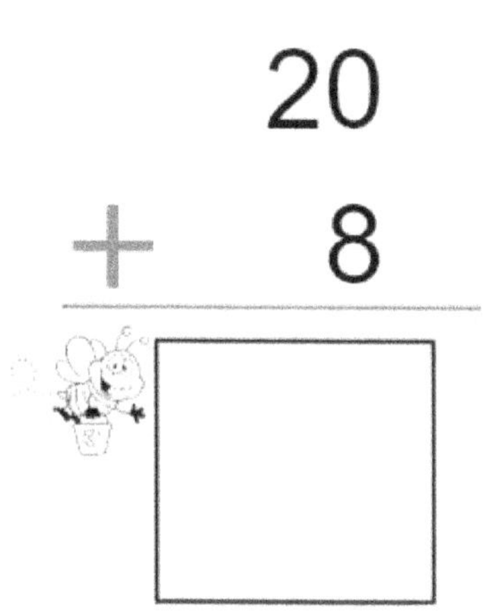

$$20 + 8$$

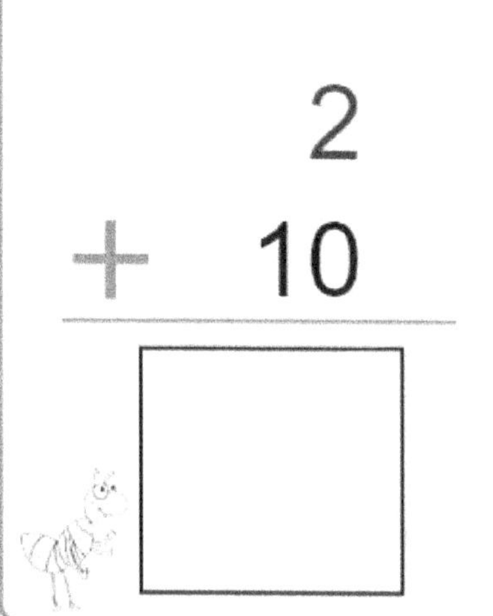

$$2 + 10$$

$$20 + 17$$

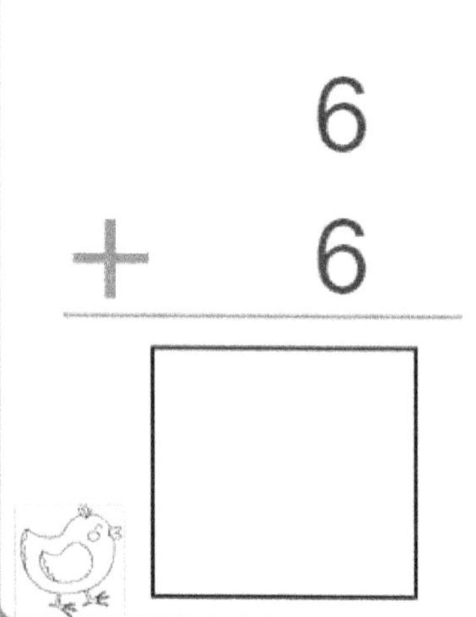

$$6 + 6$$

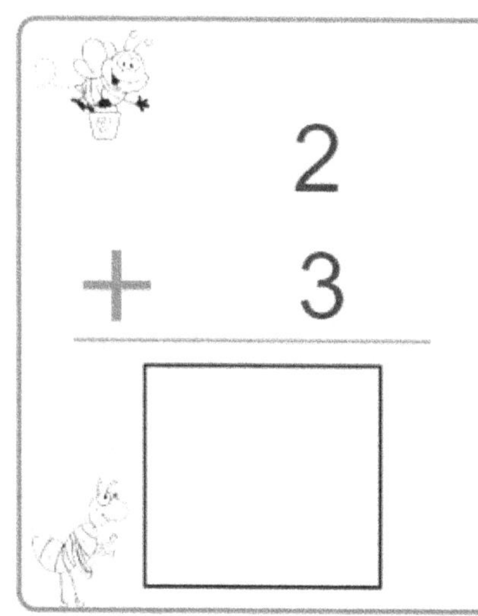

$$2 + 3$$

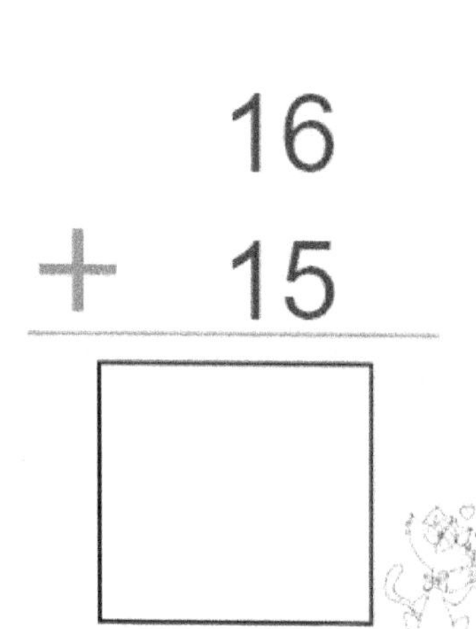

$$16 + 15$$

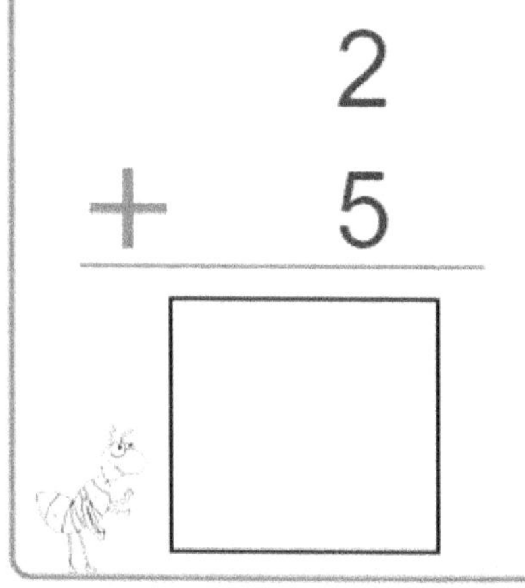

$$2 + 5$$

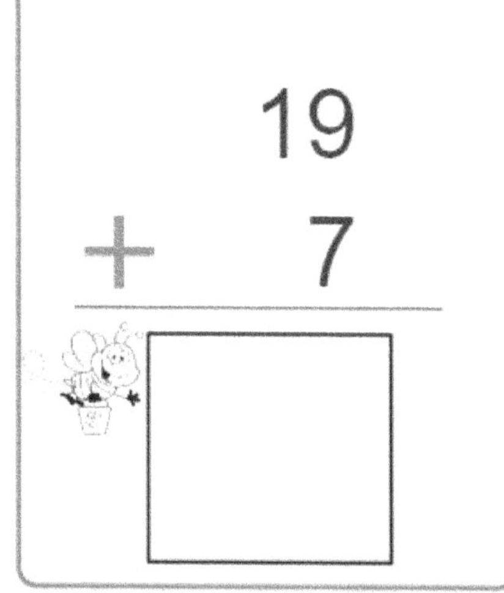

$$19 + 7$$

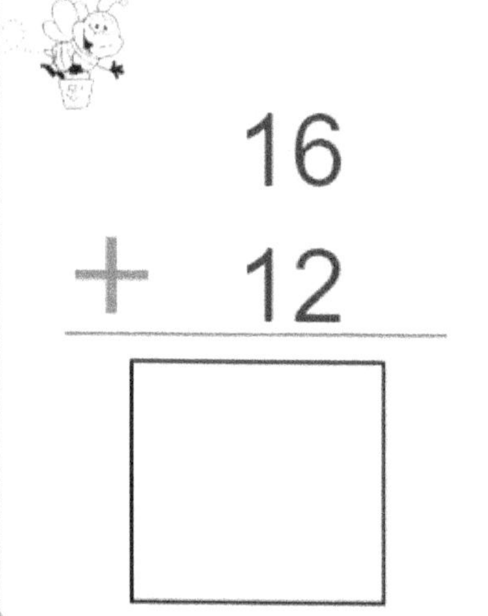

$$16 + 12$$

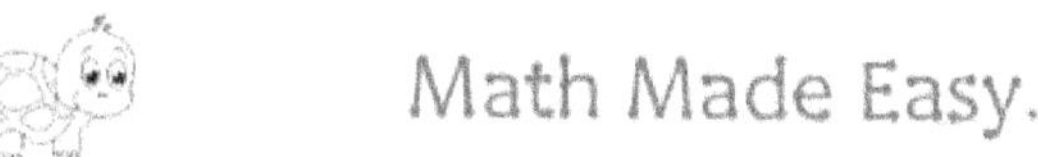

Math Made Easy....

Name : _______________________

Direction: Add the number of images in each box and write the answer in the last box.

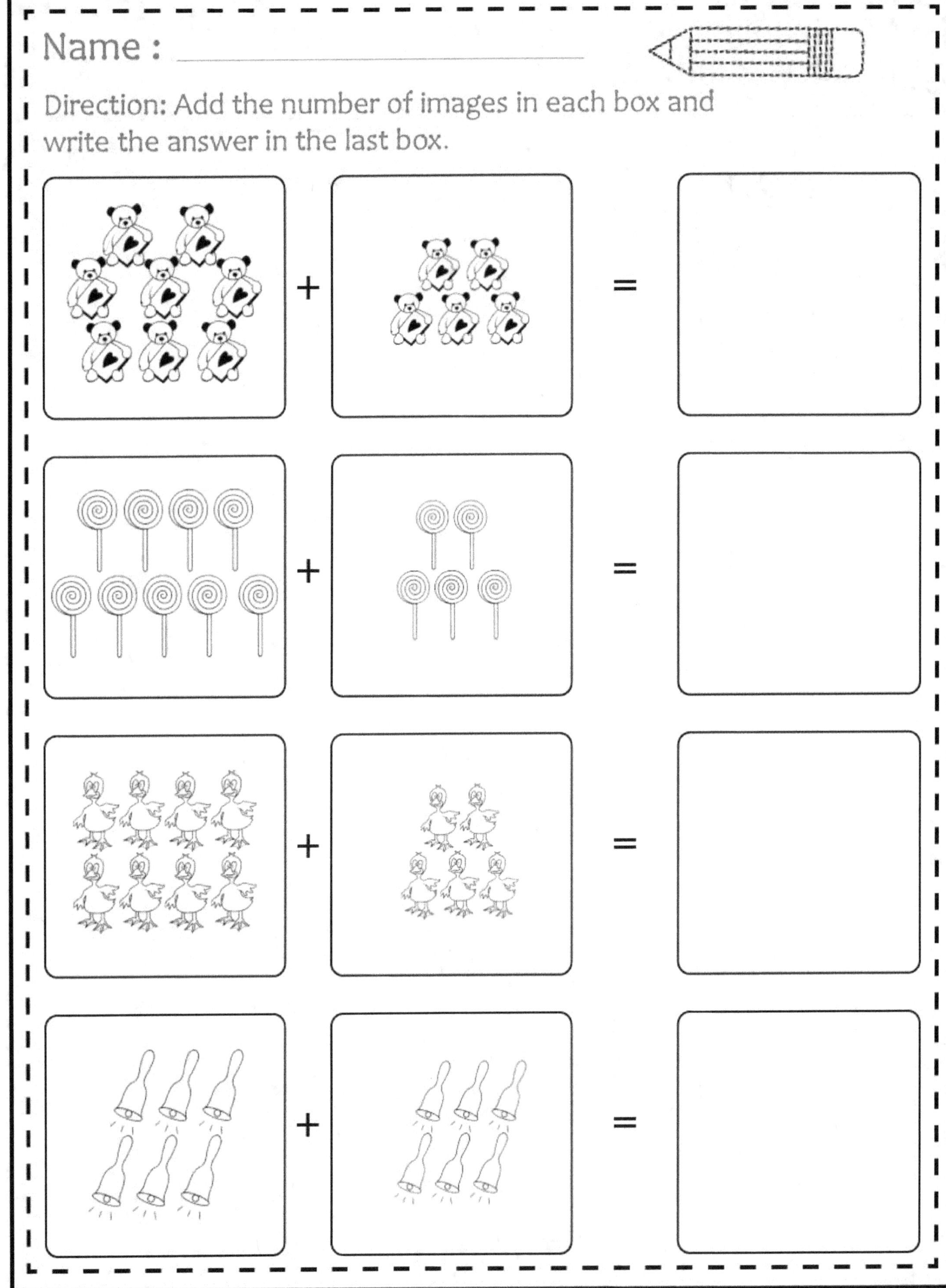

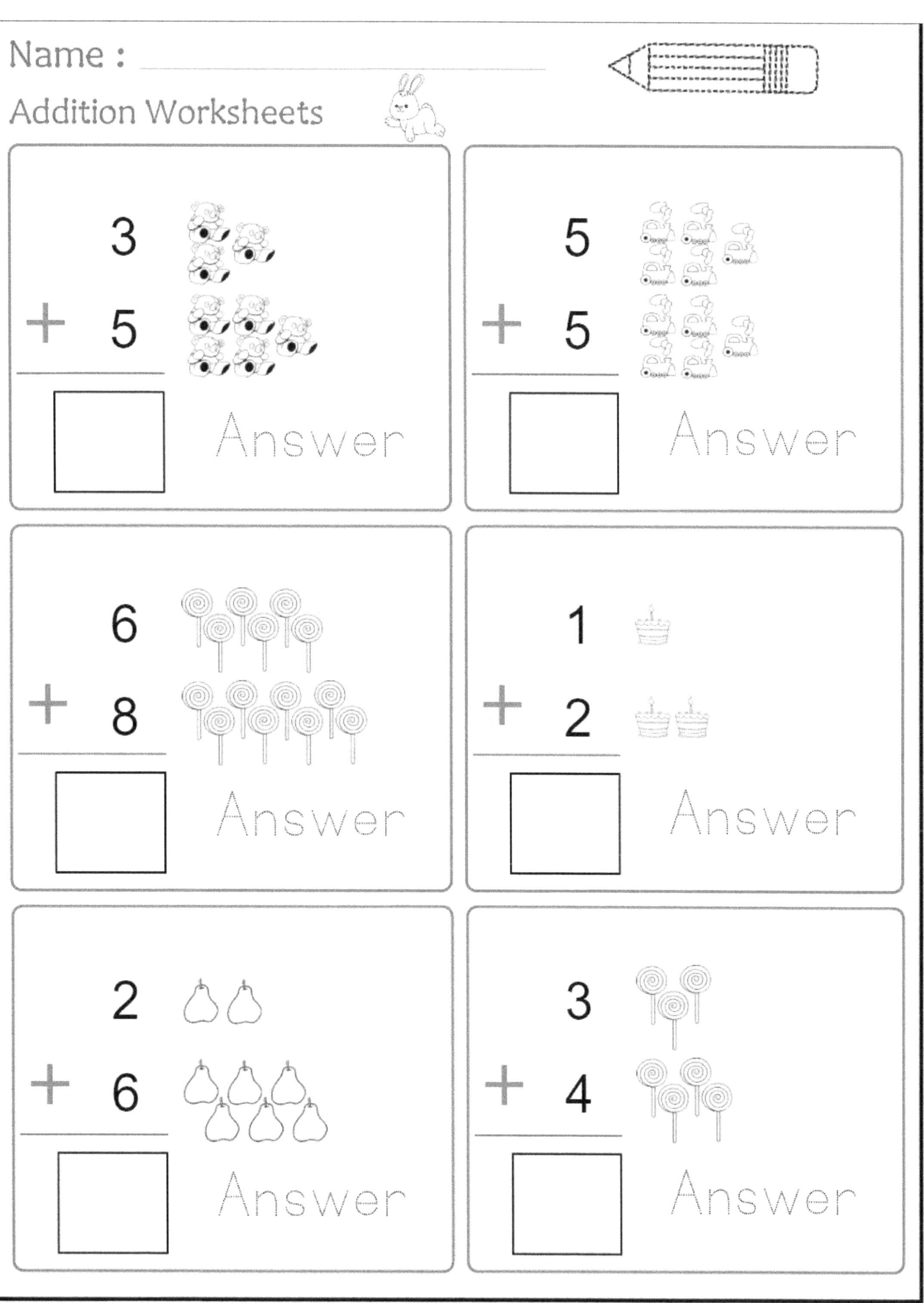

Name :
Addition Worksheets

3
+ 5

Answer

5
+ 5

Answer

6
+ 8

Answer

1
+ 2

Answer

2
+ 6

Answer

3
+ 4

Answer

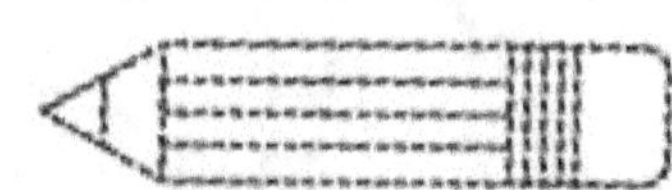

15
+ 15

17
+ 3

6
+ 11

12
+ 5

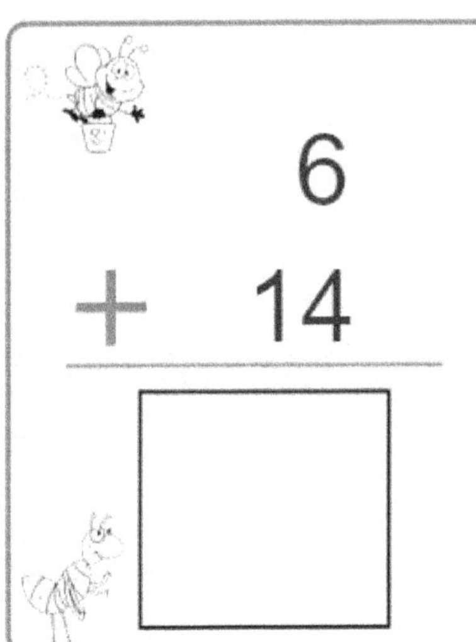
6
+ 14

1
+ 15

15
+ 3

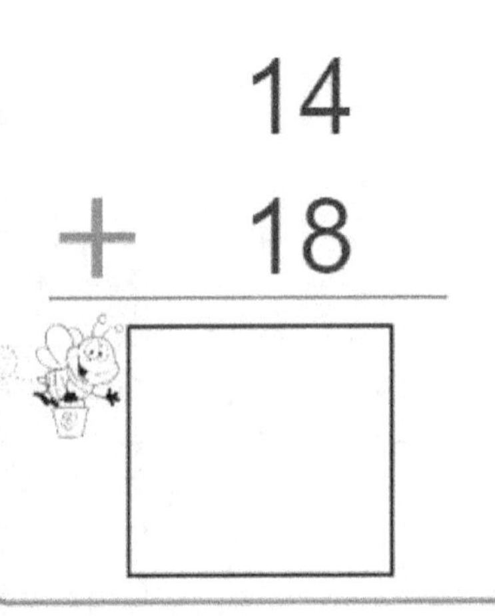
14
+ 18

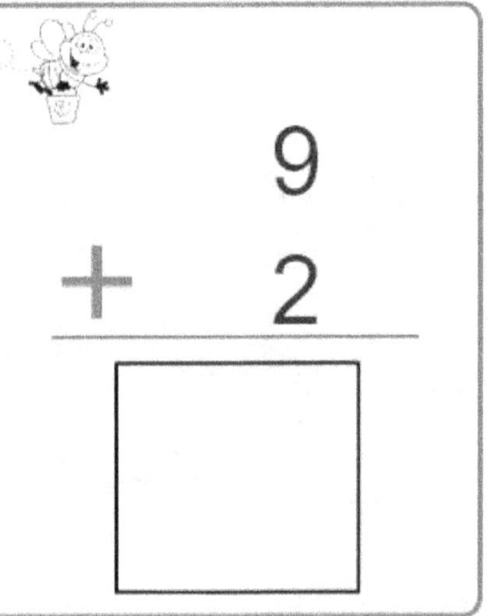
9
+ 2

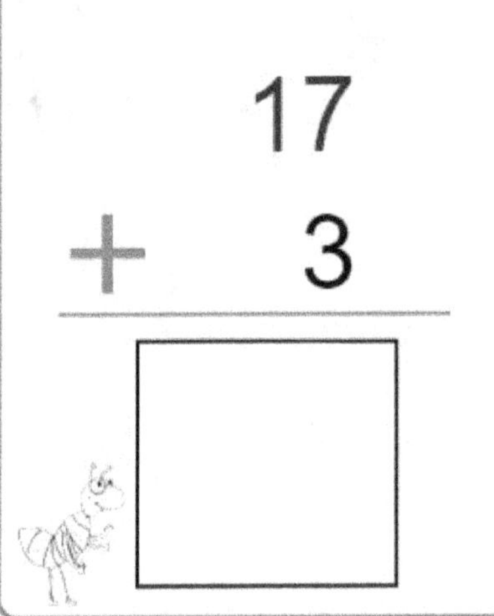
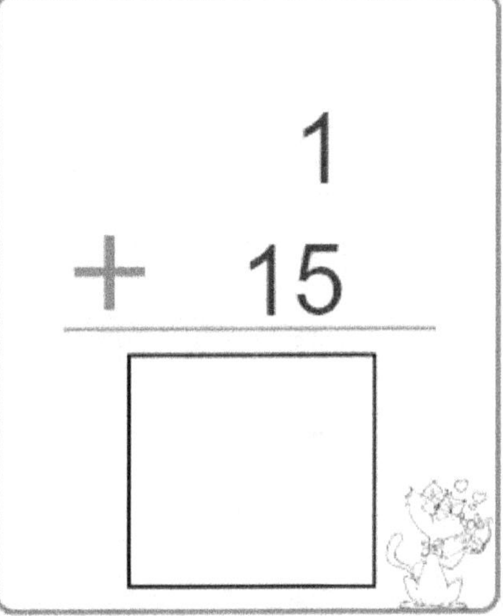

Math Made Easy....

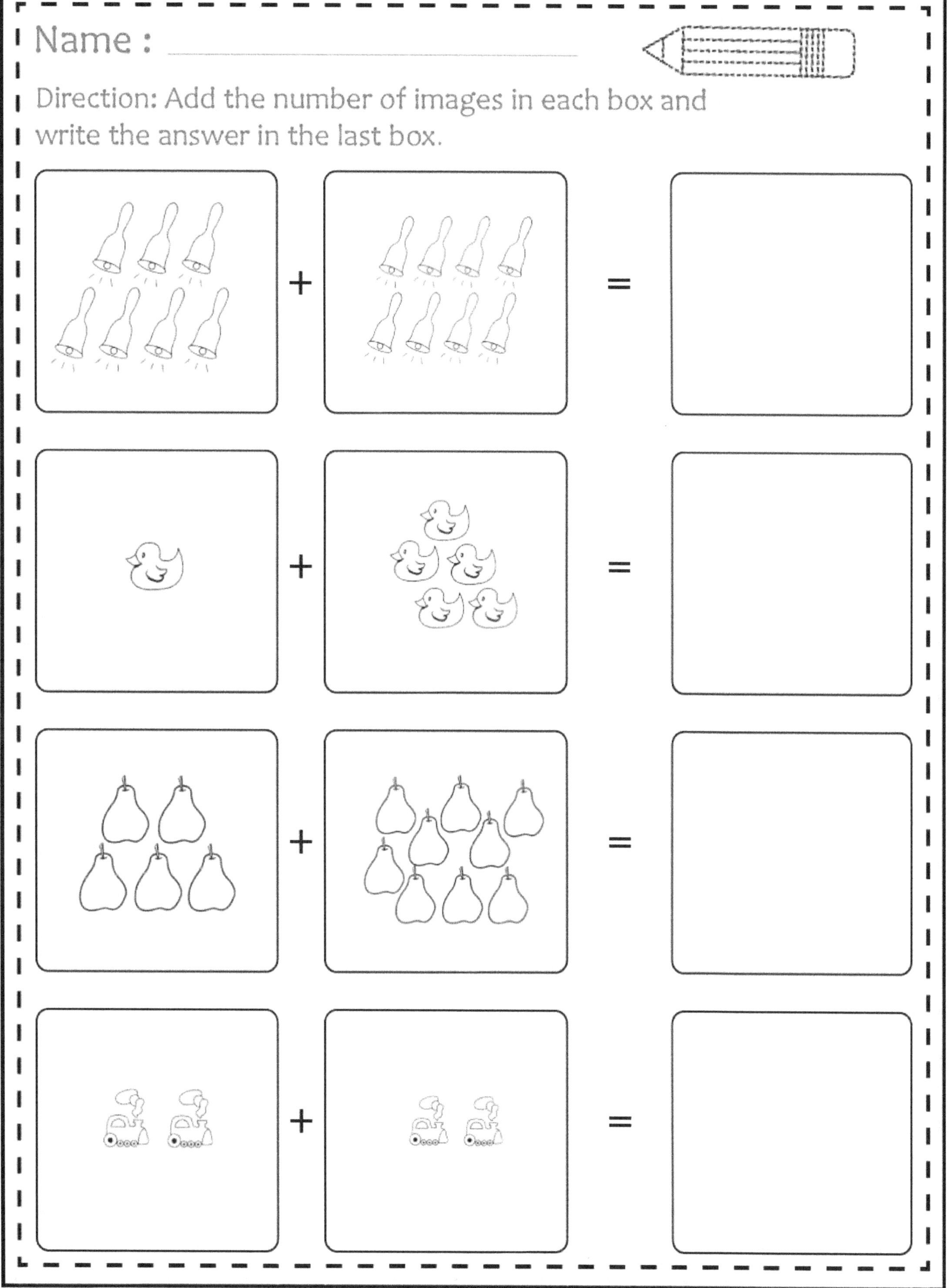

Name : ________________

Direction: Add the number of images in each box and
write the answer in the last box.

+

=

+

=

+

=

+

=

Name : _______________

Addition Worksheets

6
+ 1 

Answer

6 
+ 1

Answer

5 
+ 9

Answer

3 
+ 1

Answer

5 
+ 3

Answer

3 
+ 1

Answer

Name : _______________________

Addition Worksheets

9	
+ 19	

13	
+ 19	

2	
+ 20	

19	
+ 8	

18	
+ 10	

14	
+ 2	

4	
+ 13	

13	
+ 2	

16	
+ 2	

Math Made Easy....

Name :
Direction: Add the number of images in each box and write the answer in the last box.

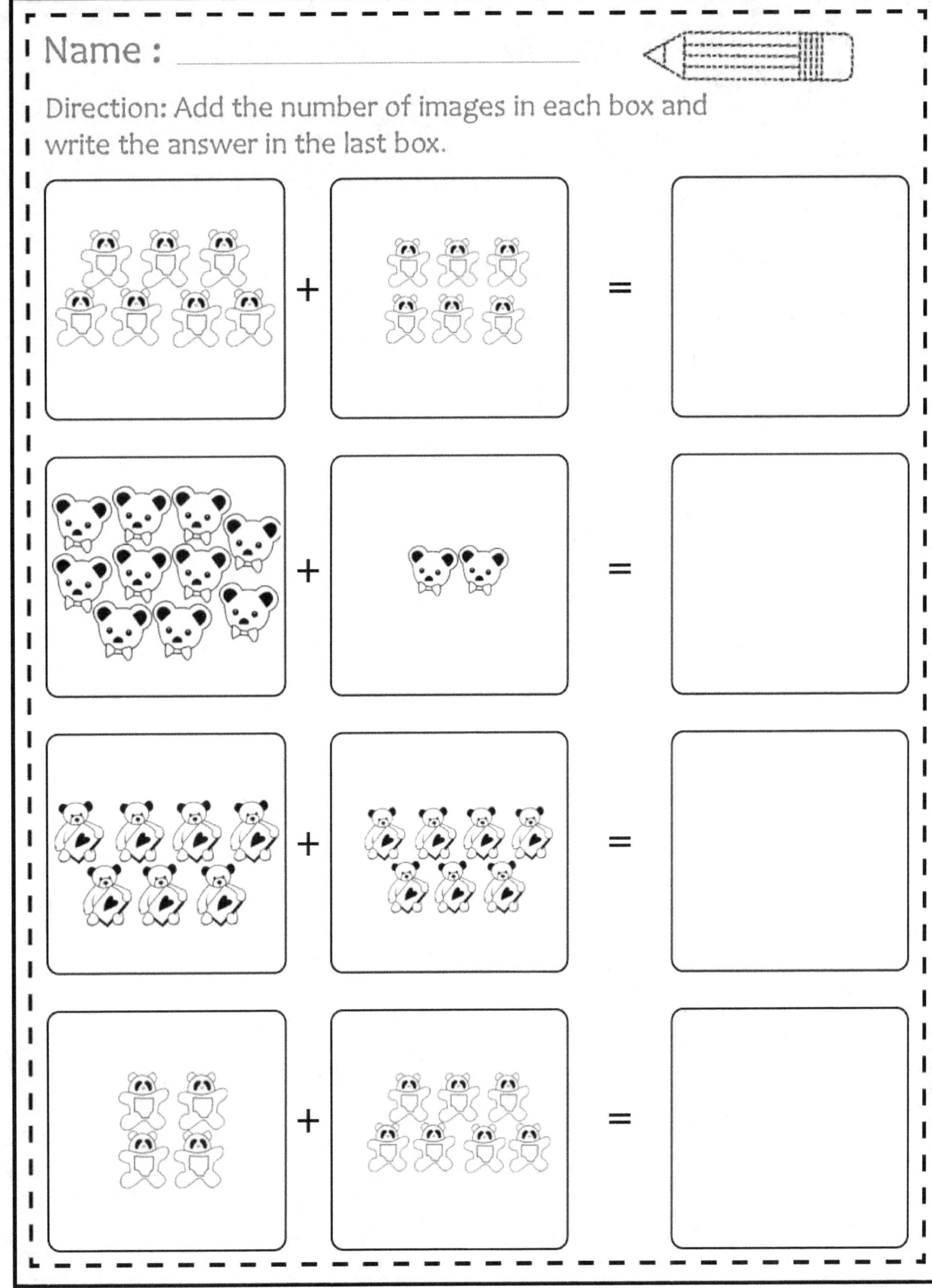

Addition Worksheets

1
+ 6

Answer

3
+ 4

Answer

5
+ 3

Answer

5
+ 8

Answer

6
+ 7

Answer

5
+ 7

Answer

Addition Worksheets

6 + 12	19 + 19	18 + 20
2 + 1	2 + 11	17 + 6
10 + 6	8 + 7	16 + 16

Name : ___________________________

Direction: Add the number of images in each box and
write the answer in the last box.

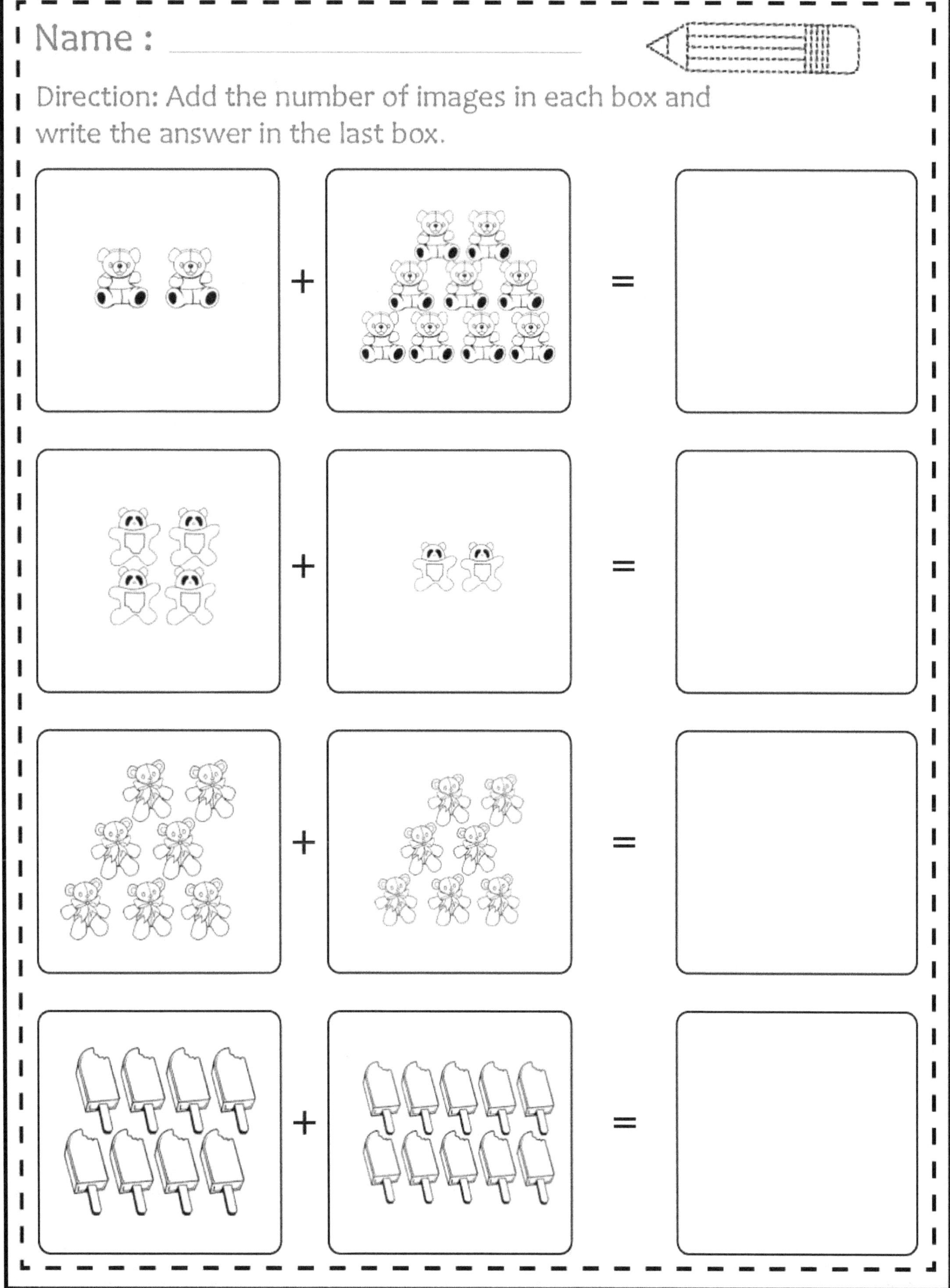

Name : ___________________________

Addition Worksheets

3
+ 3

Answer

1
+ 10

Answer

4
+ 2

Answer

1
+ 1

Answer

4
+ 7

Answer

1
+ 6

Answer

Addition Worksheets

Name : _______________

8 + 16 =	17 + 2 =	16 + 20 =
1 + 15 =	8 + 17 =	4 + 20 =
12 + 2 =	10 + 15 =	19 + 8 =

Name : ___________________________

Direction: Add the number of images in each box and write the answer in the last box.

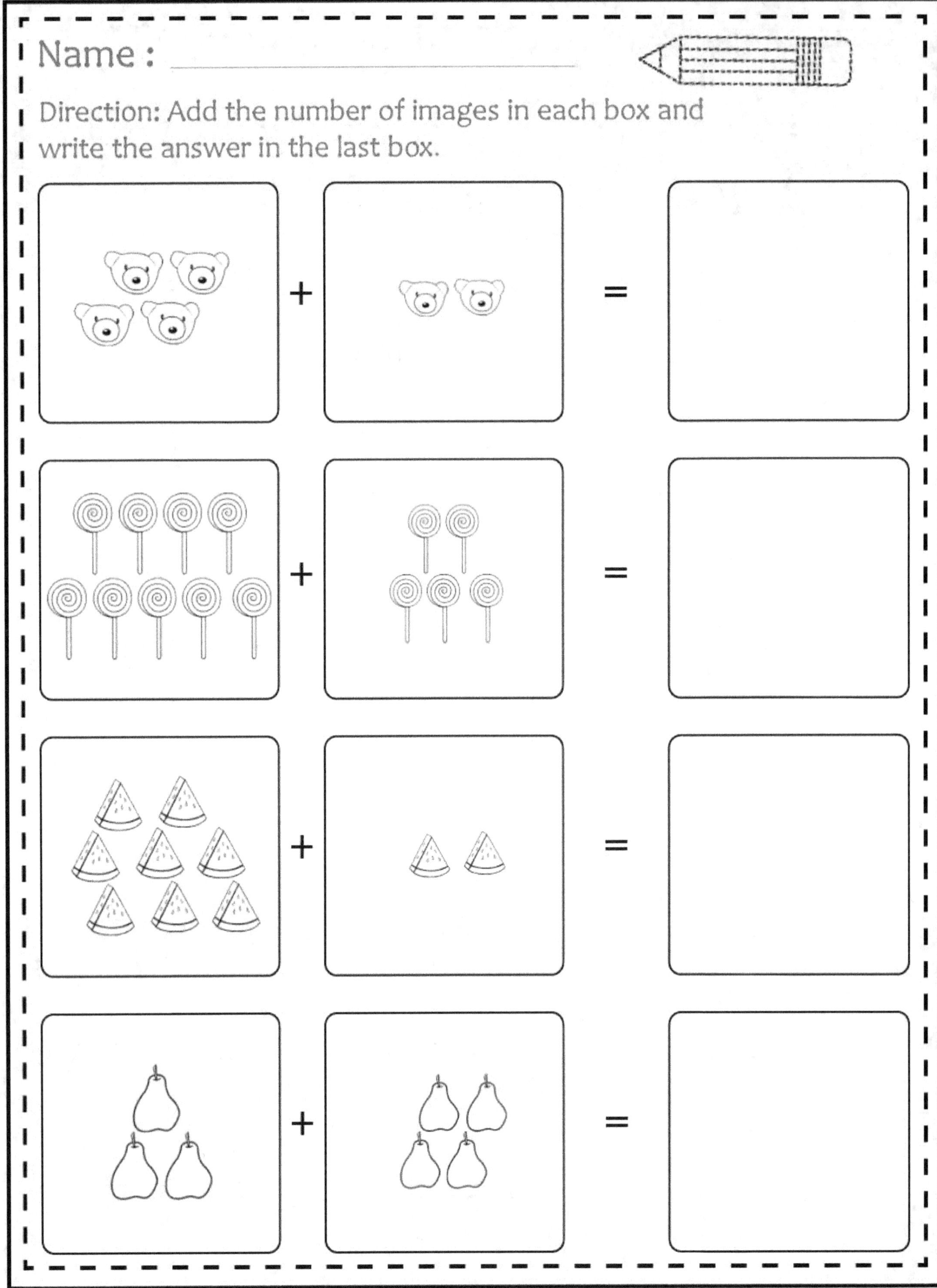

4
+ 9

Answer

4
+ 2

Answer

2
+ 7

Answer

5
+ 1

Answer

1
+ 10

Answer

5
+ 1

Answer

Name : ___________
Addition Worksheets

14
+ 7

5
+ 13

2
+ 7

8
+ 2

18
+ 5

18
+ 16

15
+ 20

18
+ 7

11
+ 20

Math Made Easy....

Name : _______________

Direction: Add the number of images in each box and
write the answer in the last box.

Name : 
Addition Worksheets

1
+ 10

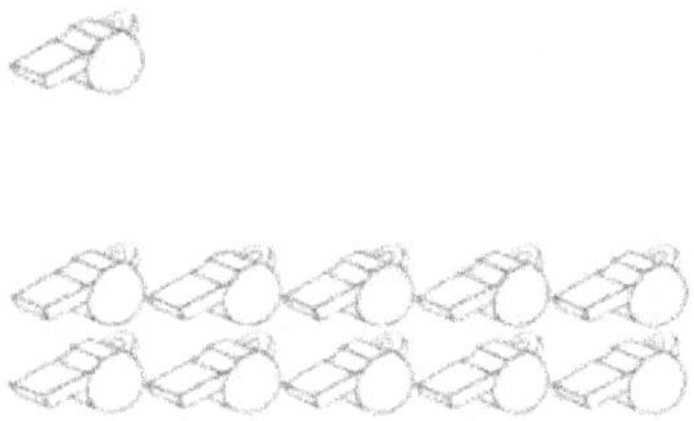

Answer

6
+ 8

Answer

2
+ 4

Answer

1
+ 8

Answer

1
+ 3

Answer

3
+ 8

Answer

Addition Worksheets

$$18 + 11 =$$

$$4 + 7 =$$

$$9 + 9 =$$

$$11 + 1 =$$

$$3 + 15 =$$

$$18 + 5 =$$

$$1 + 11 =$$

$$6 + 10 =$$

$$2 + 7 =$$

Math Made Easy....

Name : ___________________________

Direction: Add the number of images in each box and
write the answer in the last box.

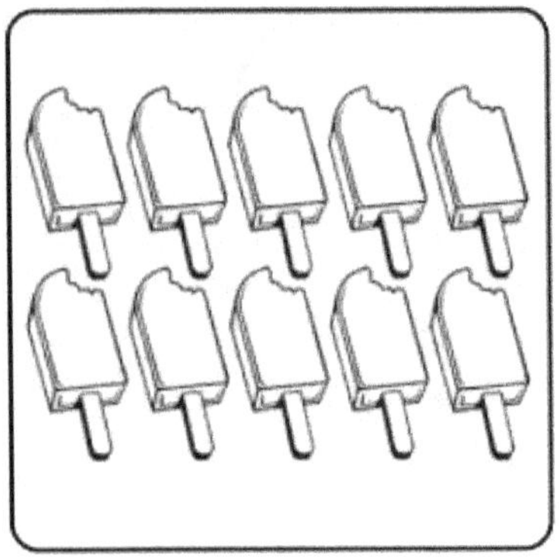

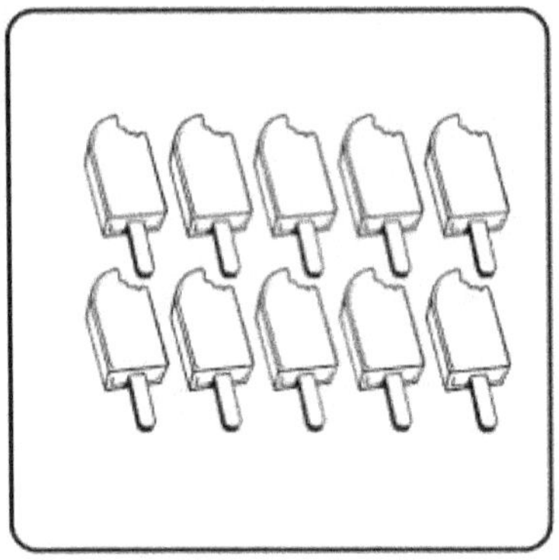

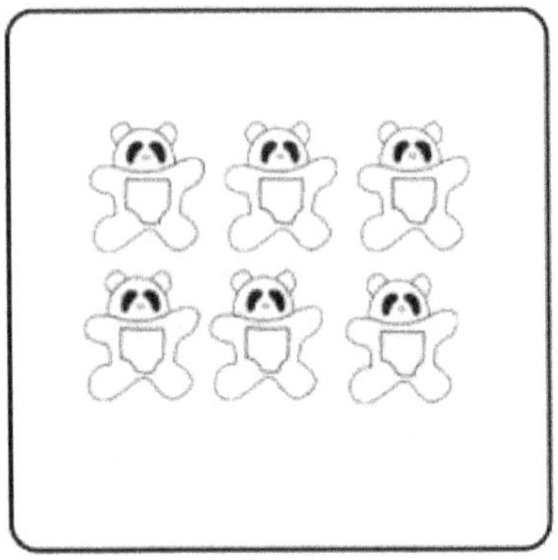

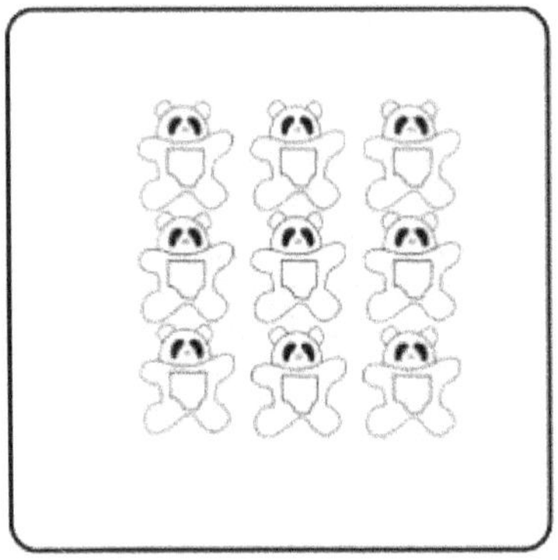

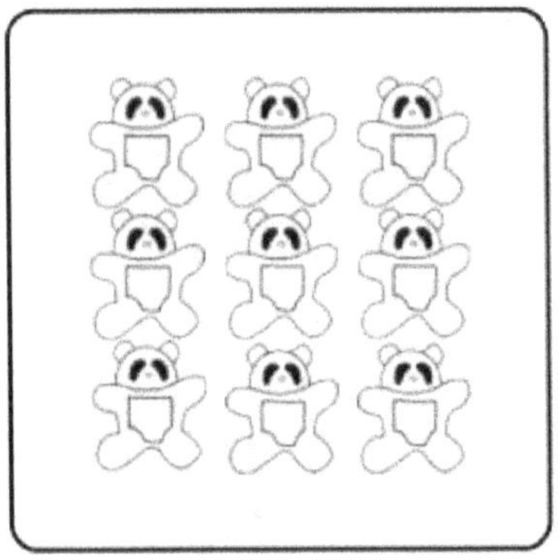

Name : _______________________

Addition Worksheets

5
+ 8

Answer

5
+ 4

Answer

1
+ 9

Answer

1
+ 7

Answer

1
+ 8

Answer

6
+ 4

Answer

Addition Worksheets

19 $+$ 7 $=$	14 $+$ 2 $=$	4 $+$ 15 $=$
3 $+$ 3 $=$	2 $+$ 17 $=$	7 $+$ 8 $=$
20 $+$ 1 $=$	5 $+$ 6 $=$	4 $+$ 19 $=$

Name : _______________________

Direction: Add the number of images in each box and write the answer in the last box.

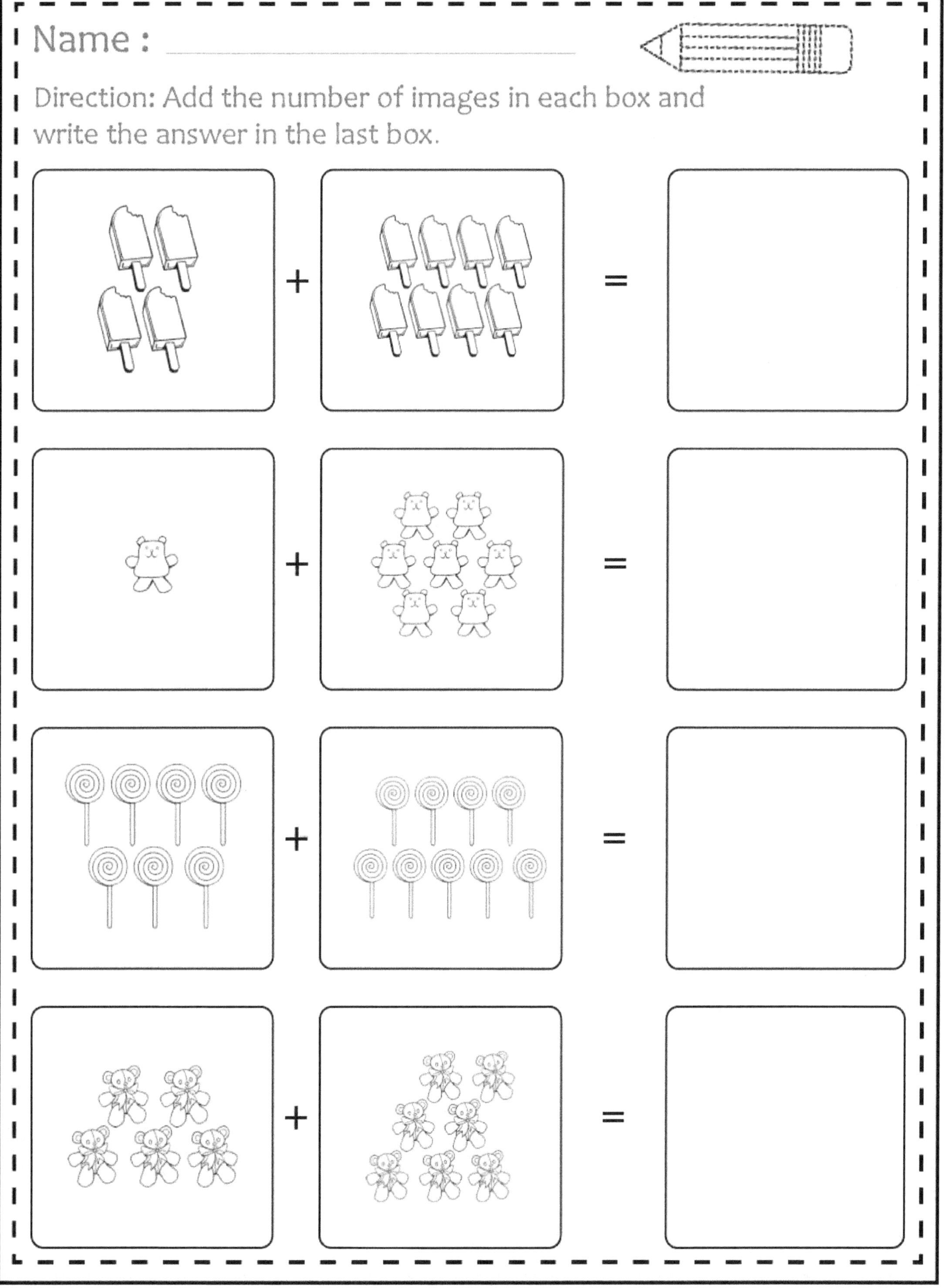

Name :
Addition Worksheets

2
+ 9
Answer

4
+ 8
Answer

5
+ 5
Answer

3
+ 3
Answer

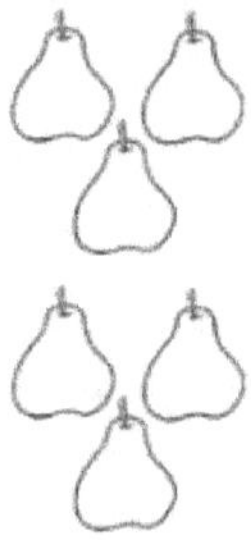

5
+ 4
Answer

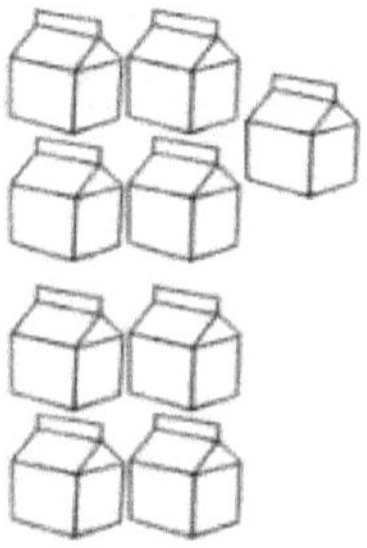

3
+ 2
Answer

Addition Worksheets

19 + 13	7 + 3	17 + 8
5 + 14	14 + 14	15 + 2
14 + 14	9 + 7	10 + 1

Math Made Easy....

Name : ________________

Direction: Add the number of images in each box and write the answer in the last box.

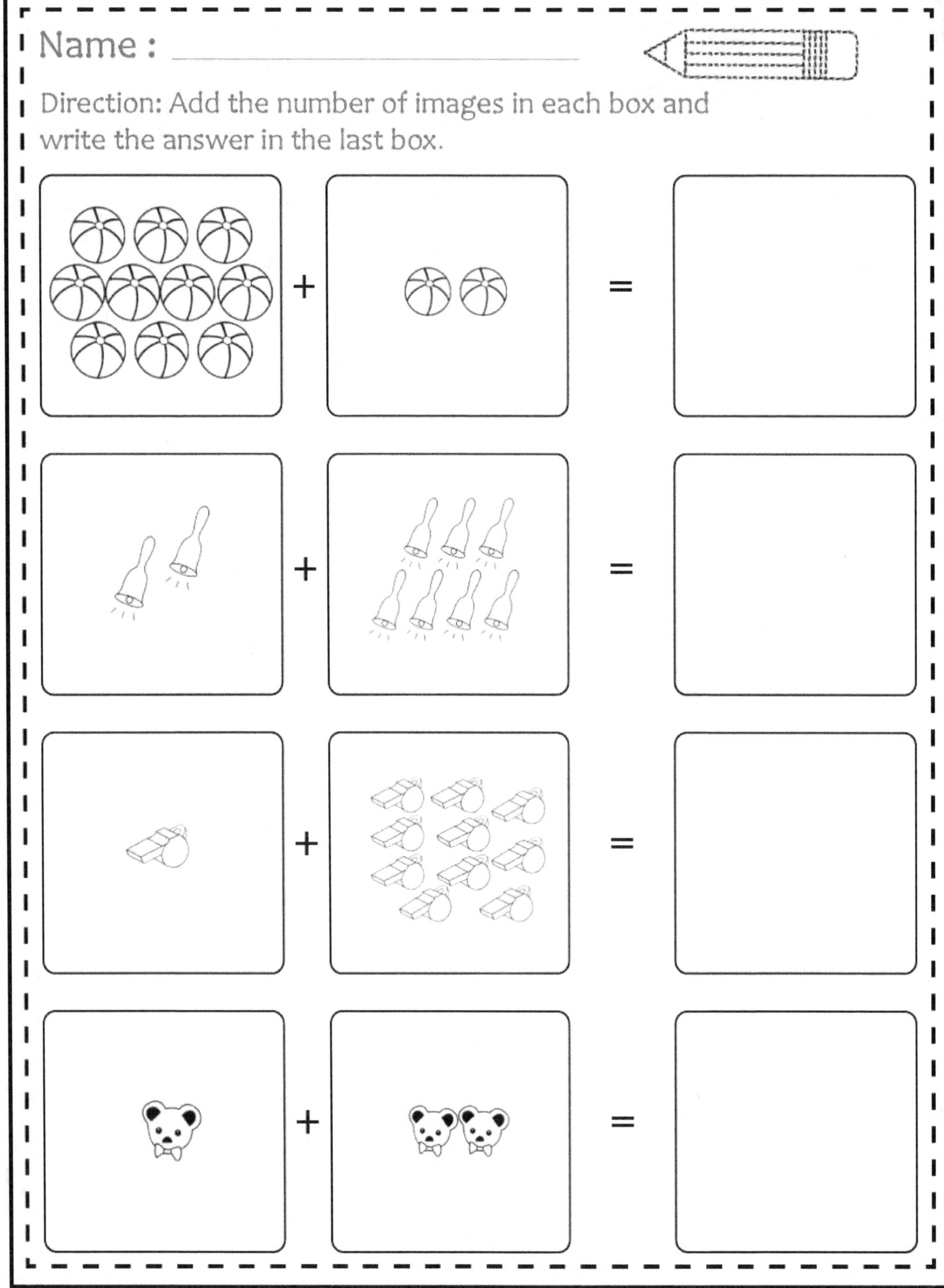

Name :
Addition Worksheets

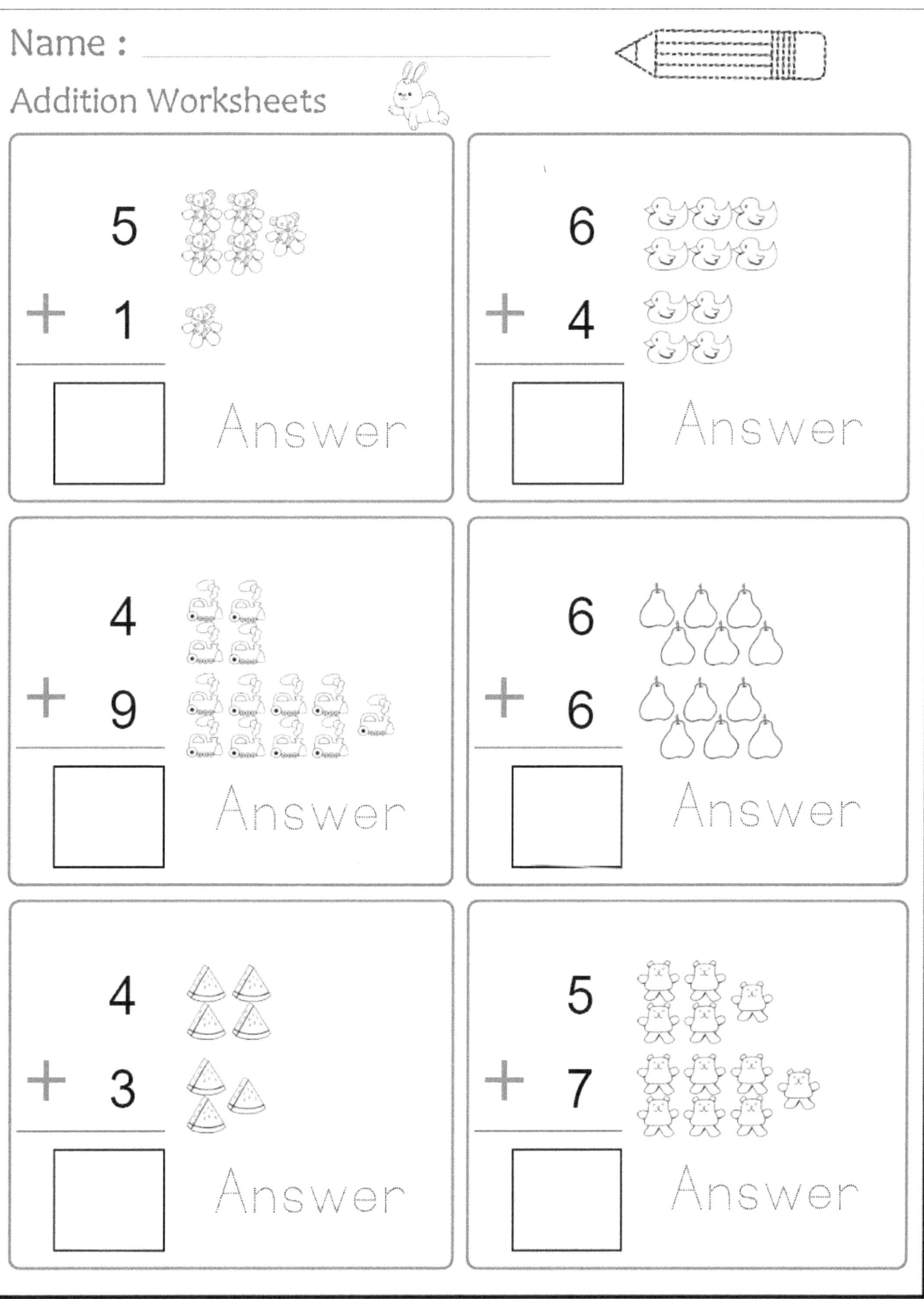

5
+ 1
Answer

6
+ 4
Answer

4
+ 9
Answer

6
+ 6
Answer

4
+ 3
Answer

5
+ 7
Answer

Addition Worksheets

$20 + 6 = \boxed{}$	$2 + 15 = \boxed{}$	$20 + 4 = \boxed{}$
$7 + 9 = \boxed{}$	$17 + 14 = \boxed{}$	$9 + 3 = \boxed{}$
$5 + 8 = \boxed{}$	$20 + 6 = \boxed{}$	$14 + 1 = \boxed{}$

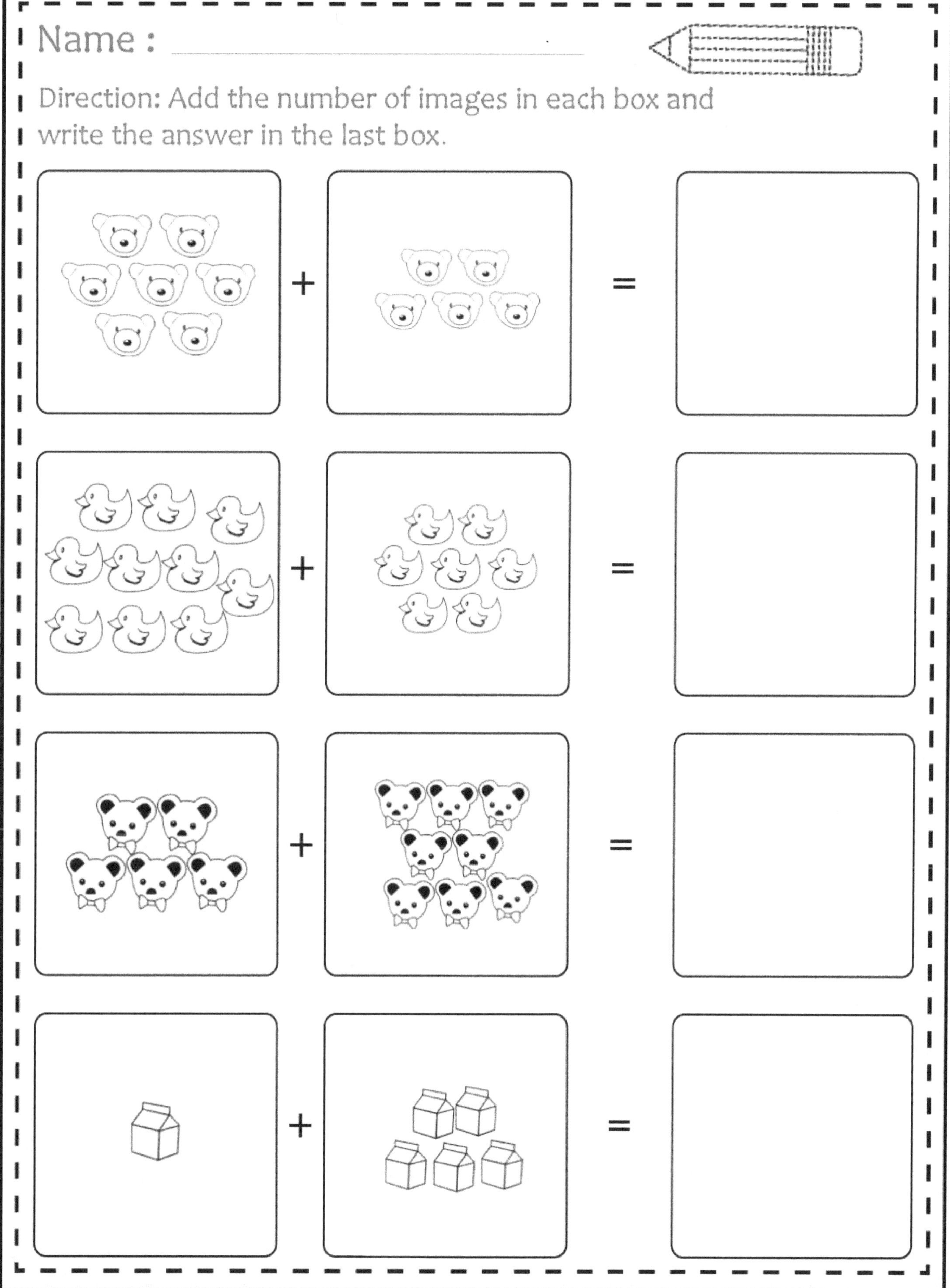

Name :
Direction: Add the number of images in each box and write the answer in the last box.
+
=
+
=
+
=
+
=

Addition Worksheets

6 + 4 Answer	2 + 7 Answer
1 + 8 Answer	6 + 2 Answer
5 + 1 Answer	6 + 1 Answer

Addition Worksheets

19 + 13	1 + 11	7 + 1
2 + 14	13 + 15	17 + 6
1 + 2	18 + 16	2 + 7

Direction: Add the number of images in each box and write the answer in the last box.

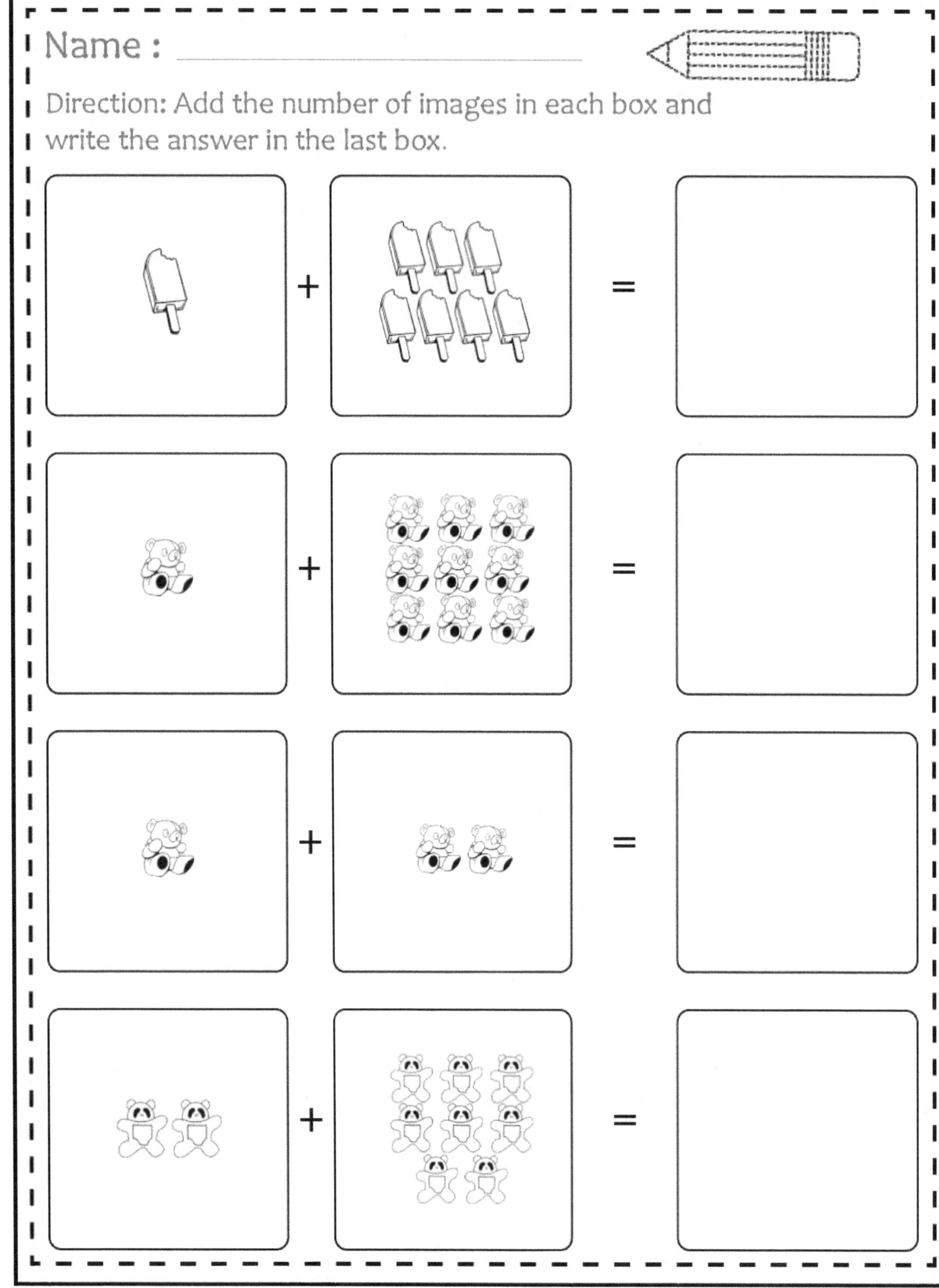

1
+ 8
Answer

1
+ 6
Answer

2
+ 3
Answer

3
+ 10
Answer

3
+ 8
Answer

5
+ 4
Answer

Addition Worksheets

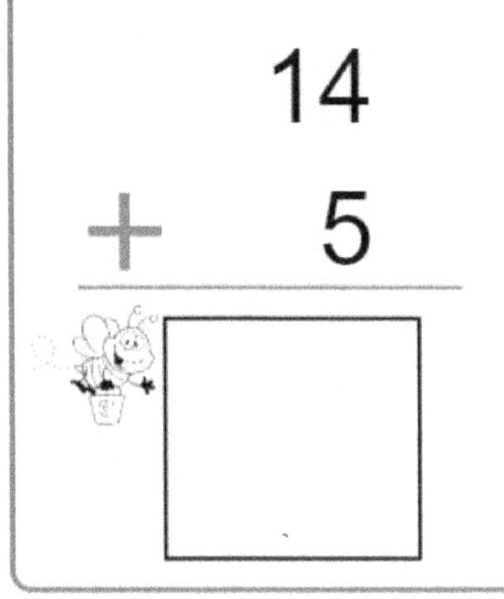

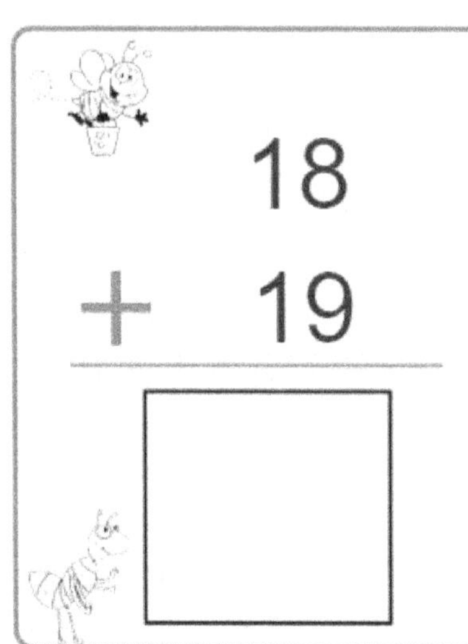

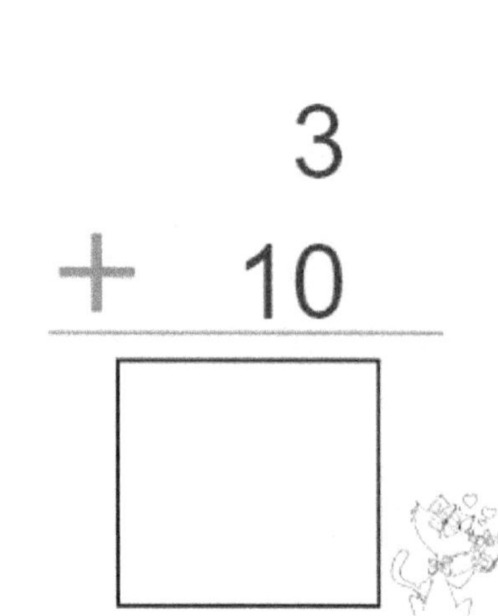

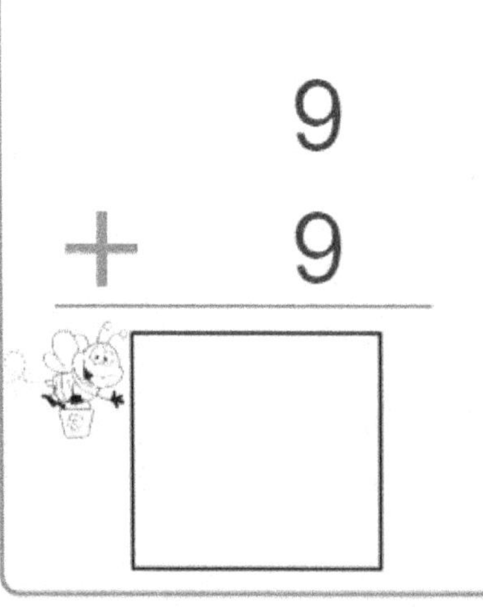

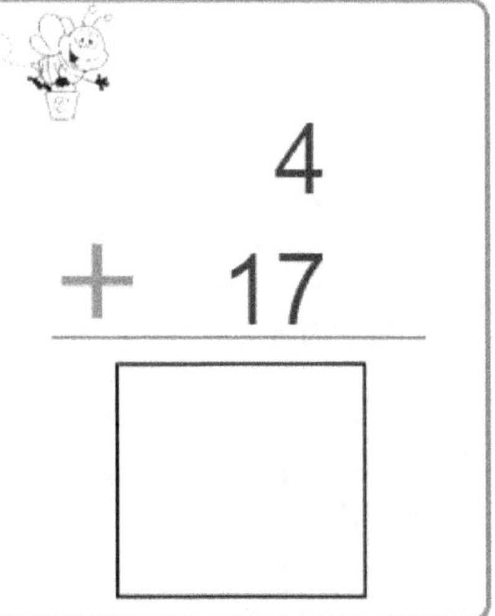

 Math Made Easy.... 

Name : ________________________________

Direction: Add the number of images in each box and
write the answer in the last box.

6
+ 6

Answer

5
+ 10

Answer

3
+ 2

Answer

1
+ 5

Answer

1
+ 6

Answer

4
+ 4

Answer

Addition Worksheets

16 + 20	1 + 19	7 + 19
3 + 9	11 + 19	13 + 10
9 + 15	5 + 20	3 + 13

Name : ____________________

Direction: Add the number of images in each box and
write the answer in the last box.

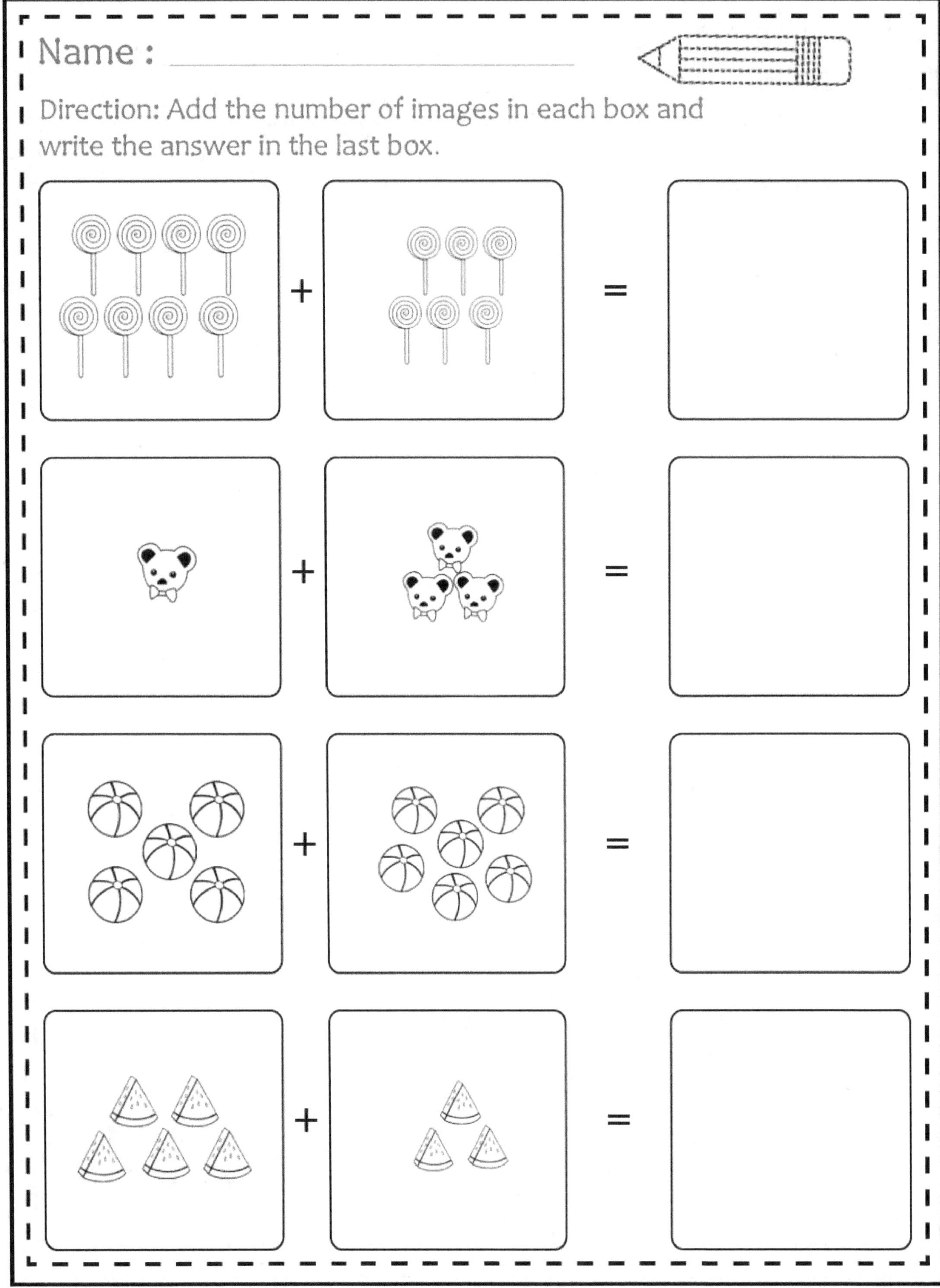

Name :
Addition Worksheets

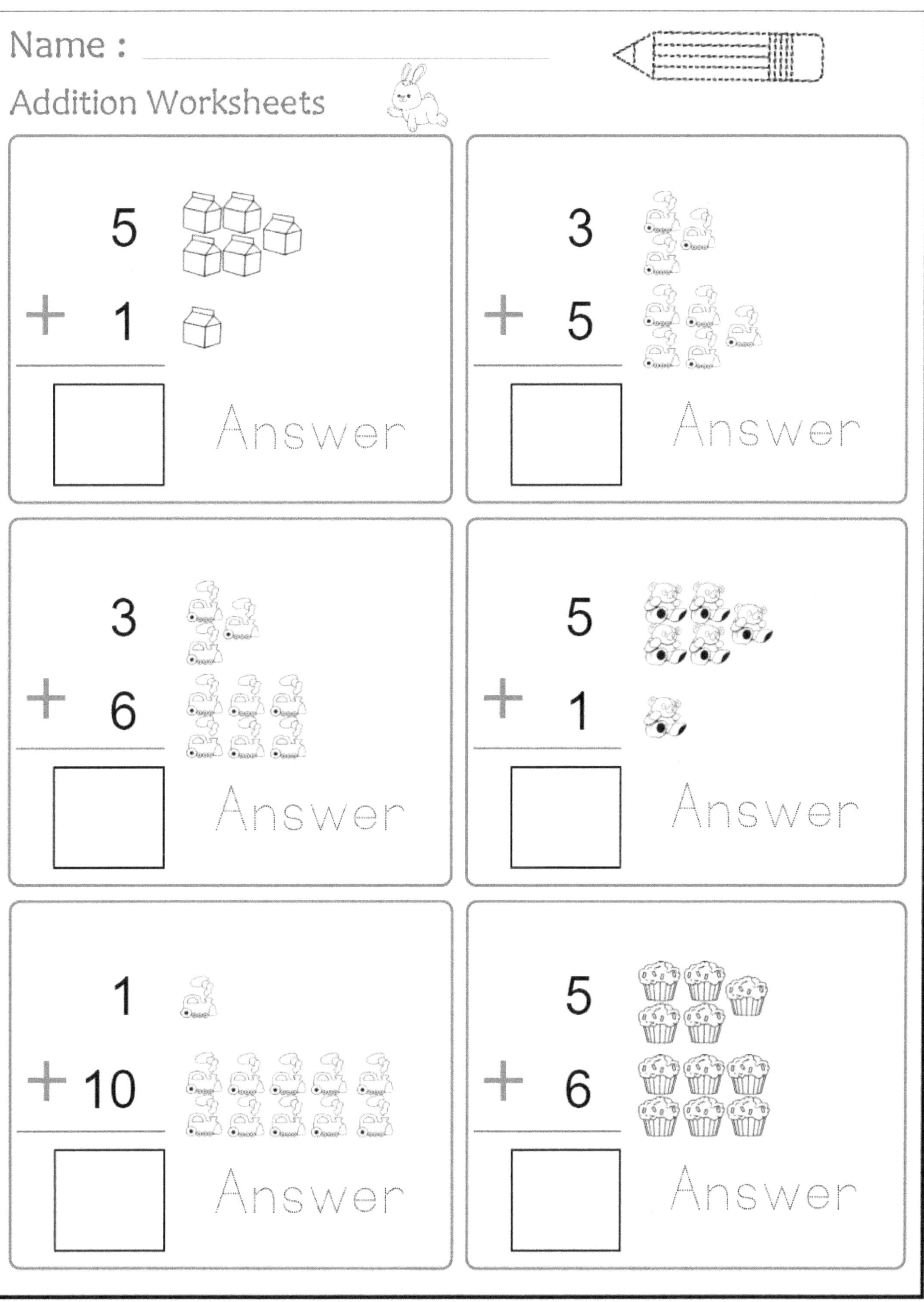

5
+ 1
Answer

3
+ 5
Answer

3
+ 6
Answer

5
+ 1
Answer

1
+ 10
Answer

5
+ 6
Answer

Addition Worksheets

5 + 15	7 + 2	6 + 1
20 + 4	11 + 1	3 + 13
3 + 9	2 + 19	20 + 12

Name :
Direction: Add the number of images in each box and write the answer in the last box.

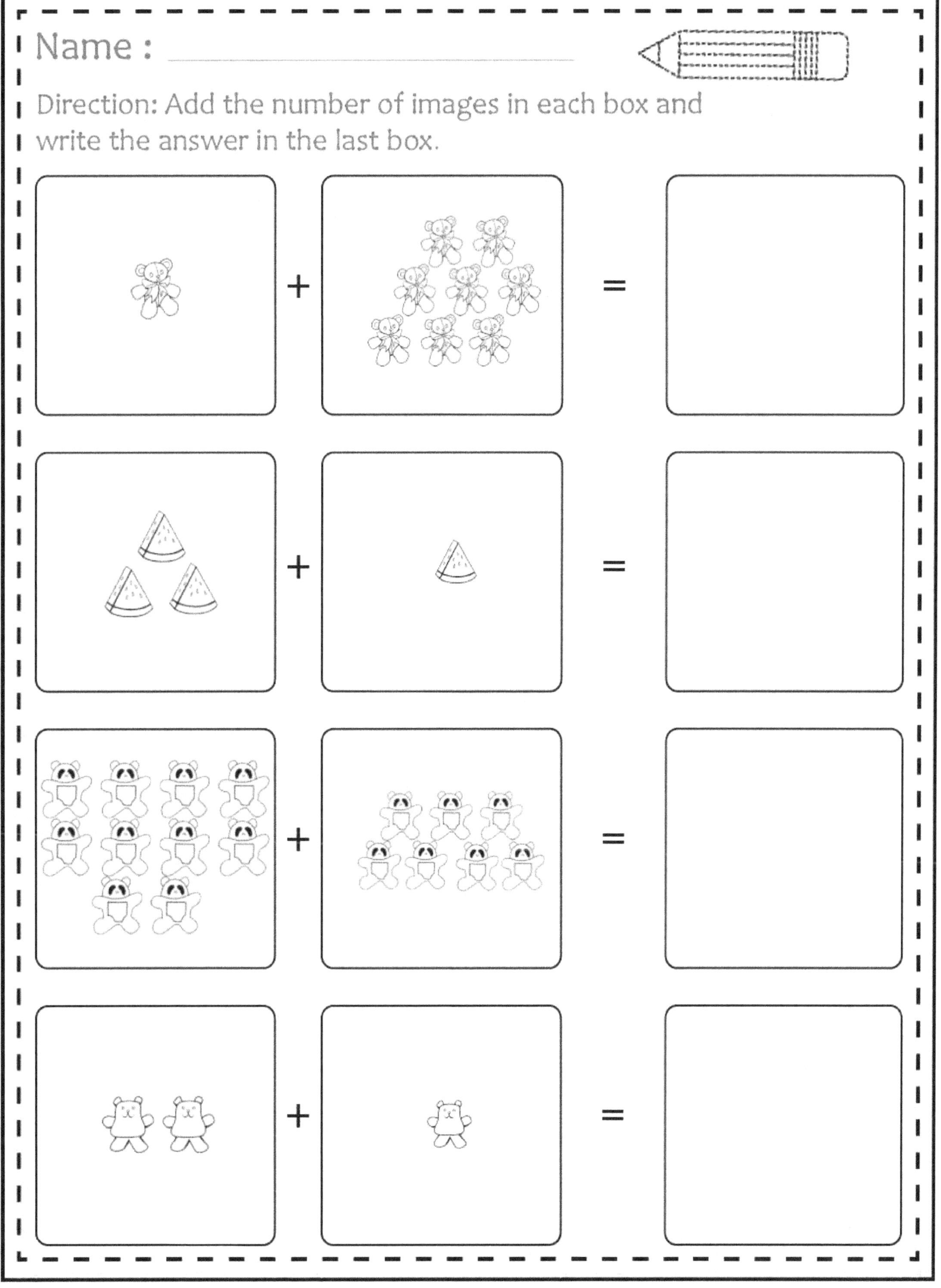

2
+ 2

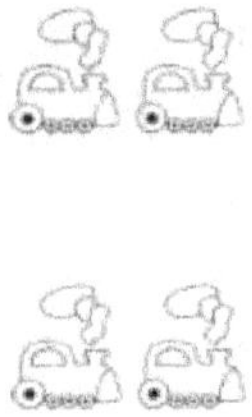

Answer

6
+ 1

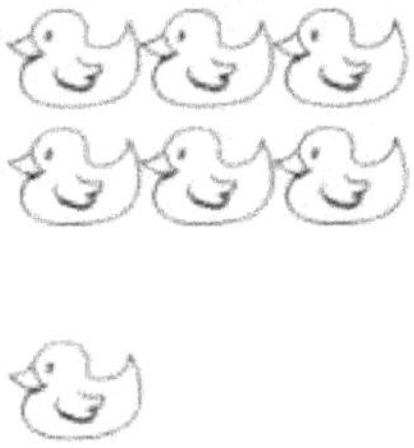

Answer

1
+ 5

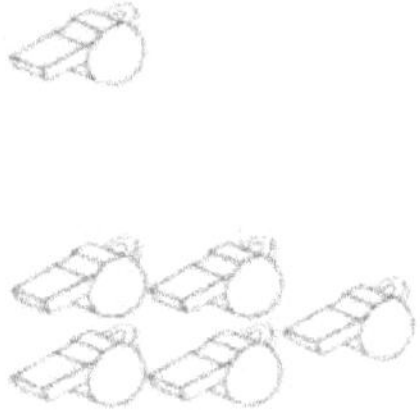

Answer

3
+ 1

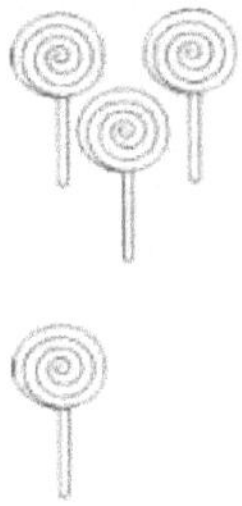

Answer

2
+ 6

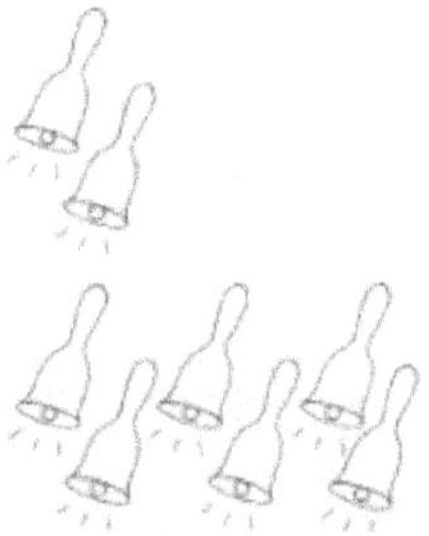

Answer

4
+ 9

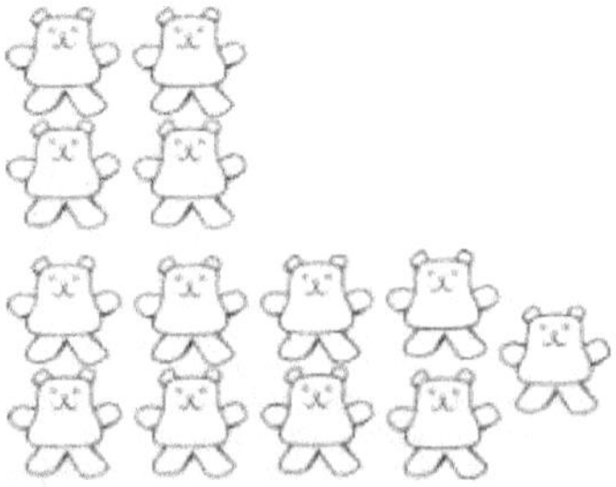

Answer

Name : _______________

Addition Worksheets

13 + 13	1 + 6	20 + 14
8 + 13	16 + 10	5 + 2
16 + 2	18 + 16	8 + 1

Math Made Easy....

Name : _______________________

Direction: Add the number of images in each box and write the answer in the last box.

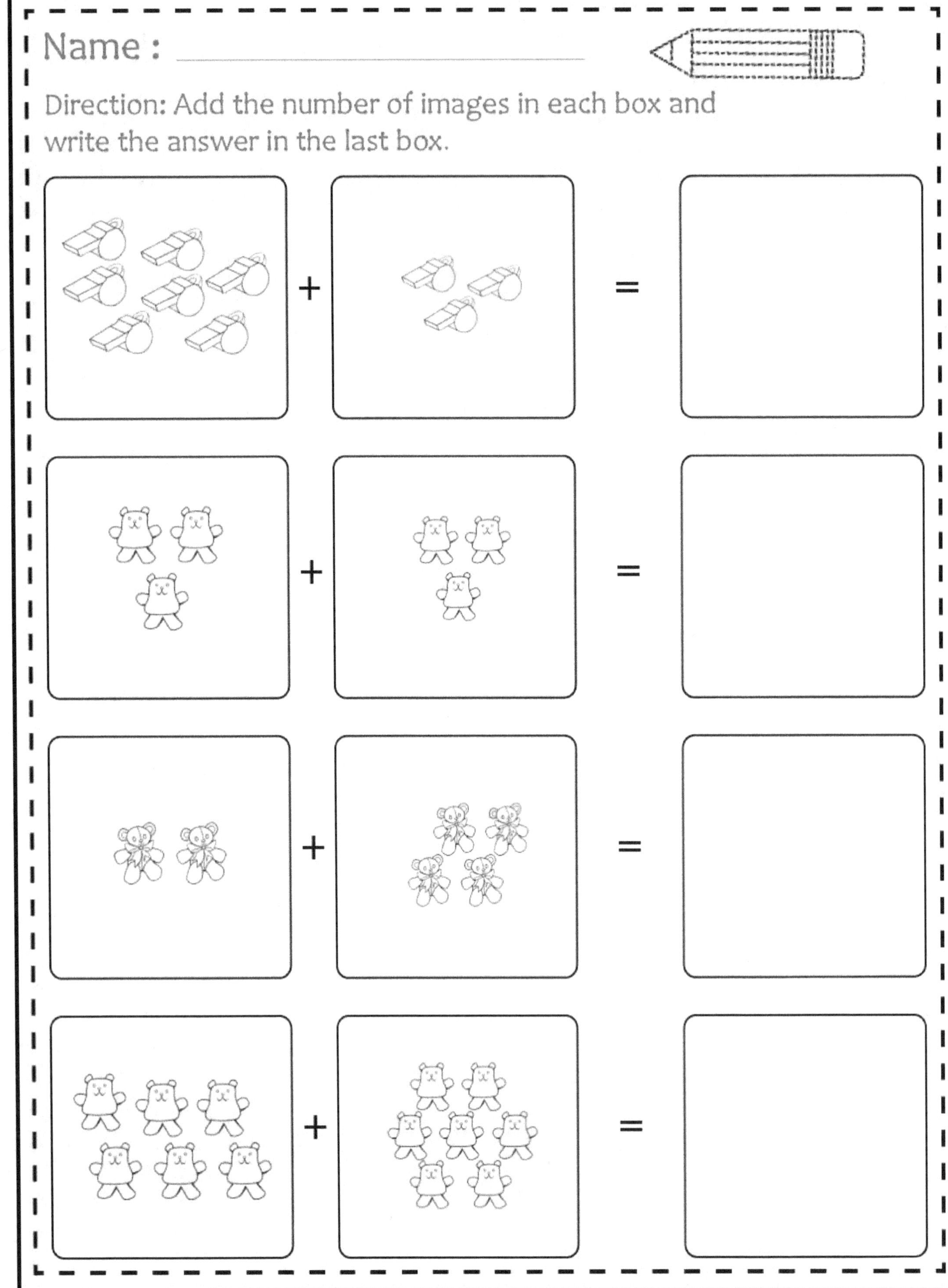

Name : _______________

Addition Worksheets

1
+ 8

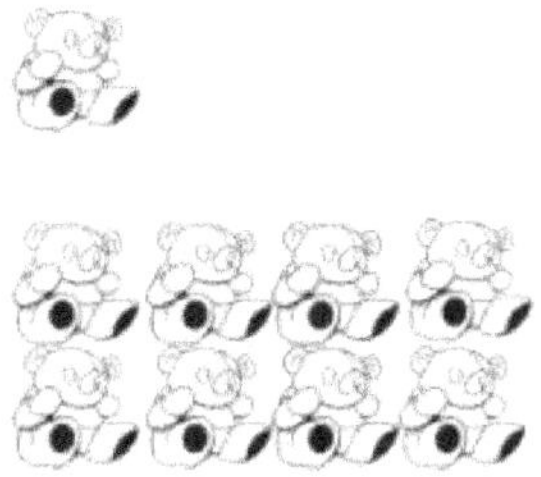

Answer

6
+ 9

Answer

6
+ 9

Answer

3
+ 8

Answer

2
+ 4

Answer

4
+ 7

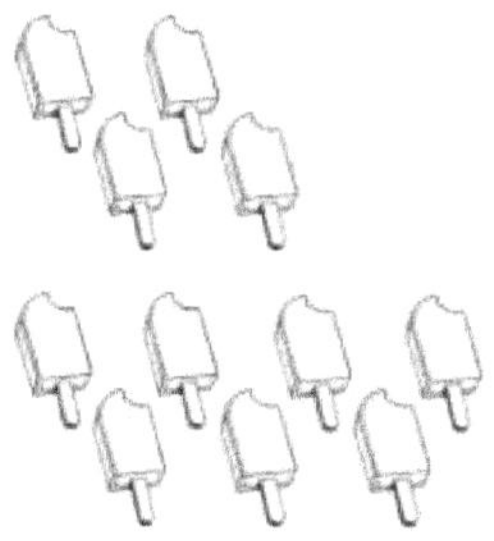

Answer